The Cycle
Of
Sin

By

Francine E. Shaw

Published by
ACTS Publishing

© 2015 Francine E. Shaw

Published by:
ACTS Publishing
P.O. Box 03600
Highland Park, MI 48203

All Scripture quotations, unless otherwise indicated, are taken from The King James Version (KJV) of the Bible copyright © 1994 by Zondervan

Bold comments within brackets noted in scripture are emphasis added by author. Take note that the name satan and associated names are not capitalized. We choose not to give him any preeminence, even to the point of violating grammatical rules.

Author: Francine E. Shaw
Cover Design: ACTS Creative Team
Editor: ACTS Editorial Team

First U.S. edition Year 2015
Publisher's Cataloging-In-Publication Data

Shaw, Francine E.

The Cycle of Sin
Biblical principles and practices for victorious Christian Living

10 Digit ISBN   0986176702   Perfect Bound Soft Cover
13 Digit ISBN   978-0-9861767-0-8   Perfect Bound Soft Cover

  1.   Christianity, Christian Living

For current information about releases by Francine E. Shaw or other releases contact: *ACTS Publishing,* P. O. Box 03600, Highland Park, MI 48203

Printed in the United States of America

V1. 02 05 2015

Dedicated

To the All Wise God, my Father, the Creator of all mankind

To Jesus Christ my Savior, and LORD

To the Holy Spirit, who has empowered me
to walk and live in the Spirit.

To my Pop, Tenzly Turner Sr.

To my Father Robert Perry, and Mother Ella Turner
who are both in the presence of the LORD.
Thank you for bringing me into the world.

To my Husband Ronald G. Shaw
who has supported me throughout my Journey.

To my Daughters, Katrina K. Lyman-Pittman,
Felicia A. Gayle and Karimeh M. Lyman

To my Son-in-laws, Anthony Pittman, and Donald Gayle

To my Grandchildren, Anthony Pittman, Donovan Gayle,
Doshanay Lyman, and Anna Pittman

To all of my Uncles and Aunts (Living and deceased)

To all of my Sister and Brothers
Especially Barbara Ann and Willie J. Lyman
(both deceased)

To all my Nieces and Nephews
(living and deceased)

To Pastor Lernard Goggans
and my New World Community Church Family

Thank all of you for molding and shaping me throughout
our many Joys and Sorrows!

The Cycle of Sin

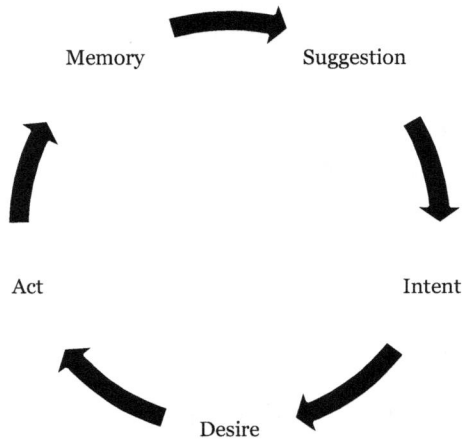

Memory → Suggestion → Intent → Desire → Act → Memory

The Cycle of Sin

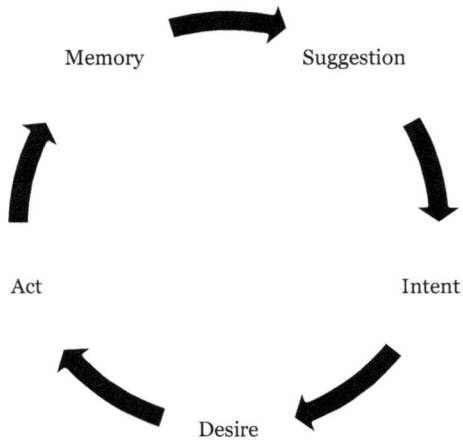

Memory → Suggestion → Intent → Desire → Act → Memory

The Cycle
Of
Sin

By

Francine E. Shaw

Table of contents

The Cycle of Sin

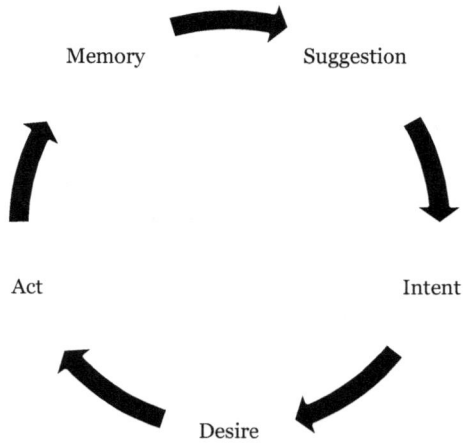

Memory → Suggestion

Act

Intent

Desire

The Cycle of Sin is the second in a series of teachings geared toward helping the believer, whose desire is to grow spiritually mature in the Lord. We grow mature spiritually by understanding and implementing the truth of God's Word in our life. *The Cycle of Sin* will help you come to know and understand that desire, initiates growth and lust hinders it (1 Peter 2:1-3).

Truth is knowledge revealed of God to mankind (John 1:1-5; John 14:6). Whereas desire, sincerely from your heart, will **enable you to seek God,** and God's will to live a holy and righteous life. Proverbs 18:1 says: *"Through desire a man, having separated himself* (from the world)*, seeketh and intermeddleth with all wisdom."* Therefore, wisdom is the ability to apply knowledge to life successfully. It basically means skill in living. The knowledge we apply to life, is the truth of God's Word. It makes the foolish, wise, and wise, wiser. Proverbs 2:6 says: *"For the LORD giveth wisdom: out of his mouth cometh knowledge and understanding."*
`

In defining the word enable, it means to provide (someone) with Adequate power, means, opportunity or authority (to do something); to make possible. When you truly thirst and hunger after the Righteousness of God, your desires will be fulfilled. David attests to this very thing, and says in Psalms 37:3-5:

"Trust in the LORD, and do good; so shalt thou dwell in the land, and verily thou shalt be fed. Delight thyself also in the LORD; and he shall give thee the desires of thine heart. Commit thy way unto the LORD; trust also in him; and he shall bring it to pass."

While in search of deliverance through prayer in 1976, I was made aware of the cycle of sin. I was also in search for the reason why? Why was I yet sinning, in spite of my desire to not sin? It was in trying not to sin, that I came to understand, the cycle of sin and was shown by God that the desire to no longer sin must go along with knowing and obeying the Word of God. So the Holy Spirit who gave me the desire to know God, placed me in God's Word, and **taught me how to become obedient.** So many of us want to trust and obey the Lord. But we neglect to study or even to read God's Word, so as to know and understand the will of God for our lives. So many of us are still walking in the vanity of our minds, and **ignorance** is what is darkening our spiritual understanding.

The Apostle Paul in Ephesians 4:17-21 says:

"This I say therefore, and testify in the Lord, that ye henceforth walk not as other Gentiles walk, in the vanity of their minds, Having the understanding darkened, being alienated from the life of God through ignorance that is in them, because of the blindness of their heart: Who being pass feeling have given themselves over unto lasciviousness, (given to or expressing lust) *to work all uncleanness* (morally defiled) *with greediness* (excessively desirous of acquiring or possessing). *But ye have not so learned Christ; if so be that ye heard him, and have been* **taught by him,** *as* **the truth is in Jesus**: (John 14:6)."

The Apostle Paul's prayer for the Ephesus Church in Ephesians 1:5-22, was for God to enlighten their eyes of understanding, so that they would come to truly know and understand the will of God (Psalms 119:18). To enlighten means to give spiritual or intellectual insight to; to give information, to inform or instruct. Truth, is what transforms and renew our minds (2 Timothy 3:16, 17). To renew means to make new, to start over; to replace. We must not only desire, but study to learn the Word of God (1 Peter 2:2). The word study means more then to read, it means for us to apply ourselves to learning; to memorize, to carefully read, to give careful thought to (2 Timothy 2:15). The Apostle Paul reveals this never ending cycle to us in Romans 7:19-20; 25, and says:

"For the good that I would I do not: but the evil which I would not, that I do. Now if I do that I would not, it is no more I that do it, but sin that dwelleth in me. I thank God through Jesus Christ our Lord. **So then with the mind I myself serve the law of God; but with the flesh the law of sin** (Romans 8:1-2).

The last verse in this passage of scripture indicates or denotes choice. This is the power we will come to know and understand in the upcoming chapters. After looking back on my deliverance, I understand now that the cycle of sin is bondage to the flesh and that the Apostle Paul in Romans 8:1-2, gives us the solution to this vicious cycle. I was able to identify five links which will be used to describe the cycle of sin.

The cycle binds us to sin by linking us to a chain, which must be broken. I was taught by God how to identify each link, and what all was involved in breaking from the cycle of sin. The links to the cycle of sin are namely suggestion, intent, desire, act, and memory. Each of the links, leads us into the next link, while referring oftentimes back to our memory. In order for us to cease from the cycle of sin, we must not give in to the lust of the flesh. We must desire and do the will of God. Our desire to do God's will, must out weight the lust factor. In order to out weight the lust factor. We must have knowledge of the truth, because the truth is what makes us free, from the bondage of sin, fear, worry, anxiety, and the cares of this world. (John 8:30-32). This never ending cycle can be broken only by the power of God, through prayer and fasting or through the obedient act, of our will. So then, knowing and obeying the Word of God is what will make us free, from the power of sin in our lives.

The intent of this book is to help you to understand, what all sin involves, and how you can overcome its powerful pervasive, and penetrating force that can master and enslave the human mind, especially when you fail to repent or to

-Preface-

acknowledge and confess your sins. It is my prayer and desire that God will enlighten your eyes of understanding, and give to you, the spirit of wisdom and revelation into the knowledge of His Son, Jesus Christ. My challenge is for you to seek the LORD, with your whole heart. (Jeremiah 29:13) Repent for the Kingdom of God is at hand!

___Introduction___

The Cycle of Sin uncovers and reveals each sequence of events we experience when we allow sin to dominate our lives. Each of the links uncovers and reveals the nature of sin, and what sin does. *The Cycle of Sin* will not only make you aware of sin, but will show you how to overcome the practice of sin in your life. Sin should not dominate the believer. But we the believer should dominate sin. We can have control of the powerful, pervasive and penetrating force of sin, in our lives. We call it self-control, it is one of the fruit of the Spirit, and is developed through self-denial. Jesus instructs us of our daily walk of self-denial in Luke 9:23:

"And he said unto them all (the twelve disciples)*, if any man will come after me, let him deny himself, and take up his cross daily, and follow me."*

Taking our cross up daily means for us to crucify the flesh and to put its deeds to death, we put the deeds of the flesh to death, by not giving in to its lustful desires. God has given to the sinner, as well as the believer, free will. We all have the power of free will, which we call choice. We have the power to choose what will become a part or not a part of our lives, whether good or evil. Sinners by nature are lost, blind, and are walking in sin and darkness (ignorance) (2 Corinthians 4:3-4). On the other hand, we who are born of God's Spirit, and are saved have a new nature, which after God is created in righteousness and true holiness (Ephesians 4:24). When you surrender your will to God, you give the Holy Spirit permission to enable or empower you to walk in the spirit, and not in the flesh.

Our walk is a spiritual walk, and requires the Word of God to grow us to obedience (Matthew 4:4). While obedience is an act of our will, what causes us to disobey the Lord is our lack of understanding of how to love, how to trust, and the lack of the understanding of spiritual things. It is call spiritual blindness, which causes us to continually walk in sin and darkness.

1

The Cycle of Sin

In 1 Peter 2:1-3, we are told:

*"Wherefore laying aside all malice, and all guile, and hypocrites, and all evil speakings, As newborn babes, **desire** the sincere milk of the word, **that ye may grow** thereby. If so be ye have tasted that the Lord is gracious."*

We all know that the Lord is gracious, but are we all willing to give up what we think is good to obey the Lord? We simply can no longer neglect the Word of God, knowing that faith without works is dead (James 2:17). God gives us grace, and the power of the Holy Spirit to overcome sin in our lives, as a result of our true desire, to please God and not our flesh.

Therefore, you and I must be doers of the Word, and not hearers only. Hebrews 11:6 says:

"But without faith it is impossible to please him: for he that cometh to God must believe that he is, and that he is a rewarder of them that diligently seek him."

Scripture let us know that faith apart from the Word of God is dead. We must know the Word, in order to act upon it, and acting upon the Word of God is what constitutes our works, which we call saving faith. Act means, to do, or to perform. It is our behavior or conduct that changes when we are obedient. Without obedience to the Word of God, our behavior or conduct will remain the same.

When you diligently seek God, it is much more than reading or studying the Word of God on occasions. It means much more than going to Bible study or Friday prayer meeting every now and then. It means much more than going to Sunday service once, or twice a month. It is a true desire that causes one to constantly seek to know the Word and Will of God. This continual seeking of God seem to be in every second, minute, hour, and moment of the day. The desire I am speaking of is a true hunger and thirst after the Righteousness

2

of God that can only be satisfied by God, as we grow spiritually mature in the Lord.

The Apostle Peter first of all, instructs us to give these things up. You cannot hold on to malice and guile, be a hypocrite, envying, while gossiping, slandering, and backbiting others expecting to grow mature spiritually.

Proverbs 13:15 tells us that:

"Good understanding giveth favour: but the way of the transgressor is (difficult) *hard."*

Favour means to help or to facilitate; and to facilitate means, to make easier; to assist the progress of (growth). A sinner naturally sin, but the transgressor's way is hard (difficult), simply because he or she are citizens of the kingdom of God, and are transgressing the law (teachings) of God.

David in Psalms 51:12-13, makes a distinction between the sinner and the transgressor when he says:

"Restore unto me the joy of thy salvation; and uphold me with thy free spirit. *Then will I teach transgressors thy ways; and sinners shall be converted unto thee. I* remember praying this same prayer to God in 1986, and God has granted it.

Scriptures says in John 8:30-32:

"As he spake these words, many believed on him. Then said Jesus to those Jews which believed on him, if ye continue in my word, then are ye my disciples indeed; And ye shall know the truth, and **the truth shall make you free***."*

To continue means, we are not to allow anything, absolutely nothing to interrupt us from obeying the Word of God, which is truth.

The Cycle of Sin

Truth is absolute, which means perfect, having no defects or faults: flawless; accurate, absolute. 2 Samuel 22:31-33 says:

"As for God, his way is perfect; the word of the LORD is tried (proven)*: he is a buckler* (shield) *to all them that trust in him. For who is God, save the LORD? And who is a rock, save our God? God is my strength and power: and he maketh my way perfect."*

Scripture goes on to say:

"There is a way which seemeth right unto a man, but the end thereof are the ways of death (Proverbs 14:12)*."*

The knowledge that makes us free from the bondage of sin is truth. It is this knowledge which makes one wise to choose what is right in the sight of God. Again, David says in Psalms 119:11:

"Thy word have I hid in mine heart, that I might not sin against thee."

In order for us to not sin against God, we need two things. We need the love and Word of God in our hearts. We need to understand that love is the factor to obeying God, intentional obedience. Judas asked Jesus a question?

"Judas saith unto him, not Iscariot, Lord, how is it that thou wilt manifest thyself unto us, and not unto the world? Jesus answered and said unto him, If a man love me, he will keep my words: and my Father will love him, and we will come unto him, and make our abode (home) *with him. He that loveth me not keepth not my sayings* (teachings)*: and the word which ye hear is not mine, but the Father's which sent me* (John 14:22-24)*."*

Jesus clearly explains what it means to love him, and the Father. **It is our obedience to the spoken Word,** handed down through the teachings of His Apostles, **which proves we love him**. 1 John 5:3 goes on to say:

   "For this is the love of God, that we keep his commandments: and his commandments are not grievous (burdensome).*"*

   We must purpose in our hearts to obey the Lord. The word purpose means, a fixed intention on doing something; or a determination. Our determination should be to please God, and to obey the Lord. Our obedience is based on our knowledge (our belief) and understanding of who God is, what God is capable of doing and what God has already done for us. It is in the Word of God where we find this knowledge and understanding. Therefore, you and I are instructed to study:

   "Study to show thyself approved unto God a workman (skilled labor) *that needeth not to be ashamed, rightly dividing the word of truth* (2 Timothy 2:15).*"*

   You will never come to know the truth, if you continue to neglect the reading, and the study of God's Word. Why? This is the intent. The aim or purpose of the devil and his unclean, wicked, foul, and evil spirits are to take your mind away from God and to draw your attention to other things such as the desire for pleasure, material possessions, popularity, fame and wealth.

Again, love is the factor to obeying God, intentional obedience. How then do we receive the love, we need to obey the Lord? Romans 5:5b says that:

   "the love of God is shed abroad in our hearts by the Holy Ghost which is given unto us."

 If you have the Holy Spirit, you have the Holy Ghost and the love of God on the inside of you (Luke 11:13). If not, you can receive Christ by faith, and be born of God's Spirit. The

-Introduction-

Apostle Paul let us know that if we are saved, we can also be filled with the Holy Ghost who is used interchangeably with the Holy Spirit in Ephesians 5:18-21, by speaking in Psalms, singing hymns, and spiritual songs making melody in our heart to the Lord; giving thanks always for all things unto God, the Father in the name of our Lord, Jesus Christ. The Holy Spirit is third in the Godhead, and scripture tells us that God is love (1 John 4:8). Therefore, His Spirit is love. In other words, we are to give praise continually to the Lord and worship God our Father, and Creator. Obedience is better than sacrifice (1 Samuel 15:22).

The Sinners Prayer: (Sincerely from your heart)

Dear God,

I acknowledge that I am a sinner in need of a Savior. I ask forgiveness of all my sins. Please cleanse me and make me whole. I believe Jesus died for my sins on the cross at cavalry, was buried and on the third day rose from the dead with all Power and Authority to save me from my sins, and in my confession, I believe am saved. Thank you Heavenly Father. In Jesus Name Amen!

__Chapter 1__

What is Sin?

"Thy word have I hid in mine heart,
that I might not sin against thee."
Psalms 119:11

The Biblical definition of sin in the Bible can be found in 1 John 3:4 and says:

"Whosoever committeth sin transgresseth also the law: for sin is the transgression of the law."

Jesus did not come to destroy the law. He came to fulfill the law. When we commit sin against God, we transgress the law also.

Jesus said:

"Think not that I am come to destroy the law, or the prophet: I am not come to destroy, but to fulfill. For verily I say unto you, Till heaven and earth pass, one jot or one tittle shall in no wise pass from the law, till all be fulfilled (Matthew 5:17-18)."

Jesus is speaking here of the Ten Commandments and the prophecies which were spoken by the Prophets. The original translation of sin means *"to miss the mark"* of God's holy standard of righteousness. We are now called to press toward the mark for the prize of the high calling of God which is in Christ Jesus (Philippians 3:14-15).

Sin from a secular perspective, is a powerful pervasive and penetrating force that can master and enslave the human mind, especially when we fail to repent (sinners), or acknowledge and confess our (saints) sins. Sin simply means

The Cycle of Sin

any action, or attitude (in heart) that violates or fails to conform to the Will of God. We sin by what we think, by what we do or fail to do. The Apostle John put sin in a nutshell when he says: *"All unrighteousness is sin* (1 John 5:17a).*"*

Sin is subtle, which means it is so slight as to be difficult to detect or to describe, operating in a hidden usually injurious way; insidious, characterized by or requiring mental acuteness, penetration or discernment. The Word of God gives us discernment to recognize our sin. Hebrews 4:12 says:

"For the word of God is quick, and power, and sharper than any twoedged sword piercing even to the dividing asunder of soul and spirit, and of the joints and marrow, and is a discerner of the thoughts and intents of the heart."

God's Word is able to separate the soul (another name for the mind) from the spirit, and the body, and it is able to discern (help us to know, recognize or understand) our thoughts and the intents of our heart. Even though sin is subtle, and proceeds from our hearts, it can to seen throughout the world. 2 Timothy 1:1-7 says:

"This know also, that in the last days perilous times shall come. For men shall be lovers of their own selves, covetous, boasters, proud, blasphemers, disobedient to parents, unthankful, unholy, Without natural affection, truce-breakers, false accusers, incontinent, fierce, despisers of those that are good, Traitors, heady, highminded, lovers of pleasures more than lovers of God; Having a form of godliness, but denying the power thereof: from such turn away. For of this sort are they which creep into houses, and lead captive silly women laden with sins, led away with divers lusts, Ever learning, and never able to come to the knowledge of the truth."

We all are affected by sin either directly or indirectly. We commit sin or someone else commit sin against us. The Word and the Spirit of God are the only two sources that can shed light on our sin.   In the account of Jesus' reproof of the Scribes and the Pharisees whose tradition was to not eat with unwashed hands, for they believed that if a man ate with unwashed hands it defiled him. But, Jesus had to explain and tell His disciples that it is not what goes into a man's belly that defiles him. It is what comes out of a man's heart that defiles a man. Jesus says:

"For out of the heart (mind) *proceed **evil thoughts**, murders, adulteries, fornications, thefts, false witness, blasphemies: These are the things which defiles a man: but to eat with unwashen hands defileth not a man* (Matthew 15:19).*"*

Sin proceeds from our heart. Proceed means to arise, to originate or to result; from the heart. David, the King of Israel penned these words in Psalms 119:11 saying:

"Thy word have I hid in my heart, that I might not sin against thee."

David gives insight into what causes us to sin against God. David says we sin against God because the Word of God is not hidden in our heart. What exactly does it mean to hide the Word of God in our hearts? It means to take God's Word to heart. It means to memorize the Word. When you memorize the Word of God, you store the Word in your heart (memory or mind), which then enable your will to act upon it.

David after repentance was able to not sin against God, because he knew and acted upon God's Word hidden in his heart, rather than sin. David was able to not sin against God, because he also had the love of God in his heart. Scripture says that David was a man after God's own heart. In 1 Samuel 13:13-14, Samuel is speaking to King Saul:

"And Samuel said to Saul, Thou hast done foolishly: thou

hast not kept the commandment of the LORD thy God, which he commanded thee: for now would the LORD have established thy kingdom upon Israel for ever. But now thy kingdom shall not continue: the LORD hath sought him a man after his own heart, and the LORD hath commanded him to be captain over his people, because thou hast not kept that which the LORD commanded thee."

Scripture also says that he loved the law. In Psalms 119:48, David says:

"My hands also will I lift up (in praise) *unto thy commandments, which I have loved; and I will meditate* (to project in the mind) *in thy statues."*

Again, the factor to obeying the Lord is love, intentional obedience. Jesus says:

"If (denotes choice) *you love me, keep my commandments. And I will pray the Father, and he shall give you another Comforter, that he may abide with you for ever; Even the* **Spirit of truth***; whom the world cannot receive, because it seeth him not, neither knoweth him: but ye know him, for he dwelleth with you, and shall be in you. I will not leave you comfortless: I will come to you* (John 14:15-18)*."* We either love and obey Jesus or we do not love Jesus and disobey Him.

Think about this, if we truly love Jesus as we say we do. We would no longer disobey (his commandments) Him? Therefore, when we do obey Him, we are in fact saying that we love Him. What we put before the LORD, we value more, point blank! The meaning of love for the world is completely different from the love of God. The love of the world is conditional, and is in fact based on the emotions which vary. But, the love of God is unconditional, and is based on a command. We show forth our love for the LORD, by obeying Him. So then, sin is disobeying the Word of God of whom Jesus was in the flesh. John 1:1-2; 14 says:

"In the beginning was the Word, and the Word was with God, and the Word was God. The same was in the beginning with God. And the Word was made flesh, and dwell among us, (and we beheld his glory as of the only begotten of the Father,) full of grace and truth."

From the very beginning God has set boundaries. In the Garden of Eden, He told Adam that from every tree of the garden, he may eat except from the tree of the knowledge of good and evil. Adam and Eve's disobedience caused the fall of mankind, and sin entered into the world. 1 John 3:8 says:

"He that committeth sin is (controlled) *of the devil; for the devil sinneth from the beginning. For this purpose the Son of God was manifested, that he might destroy the works of the devil."*

The Bible does not teach that we will not sin, it teaches us not to willfully sin. Willful sin is a purposeful or intended choice to sin, even though we know it is against the Will of God. It means that you are putting your will above God's Will. Therefore, scripture says that rebellion is as the sin of witchcraft (1 Samuel 15:23). We rebel against God when we sin. Proverbs 17:11 says:

"An evil man seeketh only rebellion; therefore a cruel messenger shall be sent against him."

The devil is the tempter and his unclean, wicked, foul, and evil spirits are tormentors. These tormentors are the same ones the unforgiving servant was turn over to in Matthew 18:34-35. Jesus is speaking, and He says:

"And the lord was wroth (angry), *and delivered him to the tormentors, till he should pay all that was due unto him. So likewise shall my heavenly Father do also unto you, if ye from your hearts forgive not everyone his brother their trespasses.* Similar, we are told in scripture that with the judgment we

The Cycle of Sin

judge others with, we shall be judged with the same measure (Matthew 6:14; Matthew 7:2). God in His sovereign authority will allow adverse situations, and circumstances to come against us to get our attention, and to turn us toward Him (Hebrews 12:6-11). But if we get our hearts right with God, it will be just as easy to obey, than it is to disobey Him.

"For with the heart man believeth unto righteousness; and with the mouth confession is made unto salvation (Romans 10:10; 1 John 1:9).*"*

We can practice obedience. When we surrender our heart to God, we give up what we want, and do what God wants us to do. How we are to live is revealed to us through the scriptures, which are the revealed will of God. Good news! God has provided a remedy for our sins.

"For God so loved the world, that he gave his only begotten Son, that whosoever believeth in him should not perish, but have everlasting life. For God sent not his Son into the world to condemn the world; but that the world Through him might be saved. He that believeth not is condemned already, because he hath not believed in the name of the only begotten Son of God (John 3:16-18).*"*

Good news!

"This is the message which we have heard of him, and declare unto you, that God is light, and in him is no darkness at all. If we say that we have fellowship with him, and walk in darkness, we lie, and do not the truth. But if we walk in the light, as he is in the light, we have fellowship one with another, and the blood of Jesus Christ his Son cleanseth us from all sin. If we say that we have no sin, we deceive ourselves, and the truth is not in us. If we confess our sins, he is faithful and just to forgive us our sins, and to cleanse us from all unrighteousness. If we say that we have not sinned, we make him a liar, and his word is not in us (1 John 1:5-10).*"*

-1- What is Sin?

Let us be reminded that our walk is personal!   Although the uncertainty of whom the author of the book of Hebrews is, the writer warns us about willfully sinning. He says in Hebrews 10:26-31:

"For if we (the people of God) *sin willfully after that we have received the **knowledge of the truth,** there remaineth no more sacrifice for sins. But a certain fearful looking for of judgment and fiery indignation, which shall devour* (intended for) *the adversaries. He that despised* (rejected) *Moses' law died without mercy under two or three witnesses: Of how much sorer punishment, suppose ye, shall he be thought worthy, who hath trodden under foot the Son of God, and hath counted the blood of the covenant, whereas he was sanctified* (separated), *an unholy thing, and hath done despite unto the Spirit of grace? For we know him that said, Vengeance belongeth unto me, I will recompense, saith the Lord. And again, It is a fearful thing to fall into **the hands of the living God**."*

Warnings are given for this reason, to prevent us from experiencing what we are being warned of. Instead the author of Hebrews, who is probably the Apostle Paul, admonish born again believers to examine themselves. He says:

"For if we would Judge ourselves, we should not be judged. But when we are judged, we are chastened of the Lord, that we should not be condemned with the world (1 Corinthians 11:31-32)*."*

He goes on to say that the partaking of the Lord's Supper unworthily without sincere examination has caused many in the Church to become weak, sickly and even to die, because they have not sincerely examined themselves. He says:

"But let a man examine himself, and so let him eat of that bread, and drink of that cup. For he that eateth and drinketh unworthily, eateth and drinketh damnation to himself, not

The Cycle of Sin

discerning the Lord's body. For this cause many are weak and sickly among you, and many sleep (die) (1 Corinthians 11:28-30)."

Keep in mind that Jesus died for the sins of the whole world. In our acceptance of salvation, we are called to repent, confess our sins, and we are to be converted (change our minds). This is Jesus speaking:

"And the Lord said, Simon, Simon, behold, satan hath desired (asked) *to have you, that he may sift you as wheat. But I have prayed for thee, that thy faith fail not; and when thou art converted, strengthen thy brethren* (Luke 22:30-31)."

The Apostle Peter, who Jesus later called into the Pastoral ministry (John 21:15-17), had to be converted even though he was with Jesus throughout His ministry. Peter had to confess his sins, for which were among them lying, cursing, and his pride. To repent is to turn from sin to God, acknowledging and confessing sin asking God for forgiveness. Conversion comes through your obedience. To be converted is to have a change of mind toward the things of God (Romans 12:1-2). Whereas conversion, is a change of mind, which results in a change of conduct or behavior. The Apostle Paul asks us this question?

"What shall we say then? Shall we continue in sin, that grace may abound? God forbid. How shall we, that are dead to sin, live any longer therein? (Romans 6:1-2)

Now that we are in Christ Jesus, we have been made alive and are now the Righteousness of God through faith in the Lord, Jesus Christ and are now called to walk in our deliverance (Colossians 1:13). We are in the world, but no longer are we of the world.

We are now called to walk by faith and not by sight. Faith is not only believing, but having trust or trusting in the Lord.

-1- What is Sin?

You trust the Lord by surrendering your will to God. You surrender your will to God by doing what you know is right, while allowing God to unfold His will in your life. To unfold means to reveal or be revealed; to be revealed gradually to the understanding. God is able to do all things, even now! Colossians 1:13 says:

"Giving thanks unto the Father, which hath made us meet (qualified) *to be partakers of the inheritance of the saints in light: Who* (God) *hath delivered us from the power of* darkness (satan's domain), *and hath translated us into the kingdom of his dear Son: In whom we have redemption through his blood, even the forgiveness of sins:"*

We are told by Jesus, to enter in at the strait gate (Matthew 7:13-14), and that the door of the sheepfold allows us to go in and come out as we follow Jesus and are nourished in preparation to go into the world as witnesses, and as we follow our Good Shepherd's directions to live a holy and righteous life (John 10:9-10). We will be blessed in our obedience (Deuteronomy 28:1-13). You and I are no longer called to walk in darkness or sin, but we are called to live a life that glorifies God. Jesus also tells us in Matthew 5:16, to let our lights so shine before men that they may see our good works and glorify our Father which is in heaven. Sin does not glorify God. Unconfessed sin causes us to feel guilt, and puts us to an open shame, because of our sinfulness. Jesus did not die for us to continue in sin. But, He died to save us from our sins, as we continue in His Word (John 8:31) and abide in His love (John 15:9), understanding that the truth will make us free from the bondage of sin, fear, worry, anxiety and the cares of this world.

In Jesus' prayer to the Father, He prays for Himself, the disciples present and for those to come. He says:

"I pray not that thou shouldest take them out of the world, but that thou shouldest keep them from evil. They are not of the world, even as I am not of the world. Sanctify (separate)

15

The Cycle of Sin

them through thy truth: thy word is truth. As thou hast sent me into the world, even so have I also sent them into the world. And for their sakes I sanctify myself, that they also might be sanctified (separated) *through the truth* (John 17:15-19).*"*

Knowledge of the truth and obeying the truth is what make us free from the cycle of sin. Therefore, we are to hide (memorize) the Word in our hearts, that we might not sin against God!

__Chapter 2__

The Cycle of Sin

*"Now if I do that I would not, it is no
more I that do it, but sin that dwelleth in me.*
Romans 7:20

What is a Cycle? A cycle is a series of events that are regularly repeated in the same order. These series of events I will call links in the cycle of sin. These links repeat themselves until the cycle is broken. A link is a single element of a chain. The chain (law of sin and death) is what keeps us in bondage to sin. Once the chain is broken, the cycle ceases unless connected again. We connect each time we commit sin. The cycle consists of five links. These links are namely suggestion, intent, desire, act, and memory. The cycle of sin unless broken by the power of God through prayer and fasting or by the obedient act of your will, is a never ending cycle.

In Romans 7:14-20, the Apostle Paul reveals this vicious cycle, explaining his awareness, and sin's presence. He says:

"For we know that the law is spiritual (law of the Spirit of life in Christ Jesus)*: but I am carnal, sold under sin. For that which I do I allow not: for what I would, that do I not; but what I hate, that do I. If then I do that which I would not, I consent unto the law* (law of sin and death) *that it is good. Now then it is no more I that do it, but sin that dwell in me. For I know that in me (that is, **in my flesh**,) dwelleth no good thing: for **to will is present** with me; but how to perform that which is good I find not. For the good that I would I do not: but the evil which I would not, that I do. Now if I do that I would not, it is no more I that do it, **but sin that dwelleth in me.**"*

We can sin so easily. For example, fear causes many to lie

The Cycle of Sin

simply because they are afraid to tell the truth, because of the consequences of telling a lie (Genesis 3:9-12). The Apostle Paul simply is saying, that sin left unchecked will cause us to do that which is wrong, no matter how much we desire to do right, and unless we are conscious of our moral compass and or we are walking in the spirit, or according to the Spirit of God, we will remain in bondage to the cycle of sin. God wants your walk to become consistent with the truth of His Word. God is calling us the believers to faithfulness.

Sin should not dominate us. But, we should know and understand, that we all have a besetting sin, a sin that we seem to not be able to overcome. Know that when you do overcome this sin, speaking of the practice. The rest will become easier to break. Based on your understanding that obedience is intentional, which means done by intention, and intention is an aim that guides action. We should obey the Lord on purpose. The Apostle Paul in Hebrews 12:1-2 says:

*"Wherefore seeing we also are compassed about with so great a cloud of witnesses, **let us lay aside every weight, and the sin which doeth so easily beset us,** and let us run with **patience** the race that is before us, Looking unto Jesus the author and finisher of our faith; who for the joy that was set before him endured the cross, despising the shame, and is set down at the right hand of the throne of God."*

He goes on to say in Hebrew 4:14-16:

"Seeing then that we have a great high priest, that is passed into the heavens, Jesus the son of God, let us hold fast our profession (faith). *For we have not an high priest which cannot be touched with the* feeling of our infirmities; *but was in all points tempted* (Matthew 4:1-11) *like as we are, yet without sin. Let us therefore come boldly unto the throne of grace to help in time of need."*

Prayer is very important, when it comes to overcoming sin.

-2- The Cycle of Sin

Through sincere prayer, you will receive strength and power, to overcome the bondage of sin in your life. In Hebrews 4:14-16, the Apostle Paul tells us to lay aside every weight, and the sin which does so easily beset us, and for us to come boldly to the throne of grace for help in time of need. We are to come believing God to give us the strength and the power we need, to act upon His Word, in obedience to the LORD.

What are weights? Weights are the things which hinder the Spirit of God in the believer's life, such as smoking, drinking, fear and cursing. First of all, smoking hinders the Spirit in the believer's life by giving us a false sense of comfort. Jesus told His disciples, I will not leave you comfortless. I will send the comforter, which is the Holy Spirit (John 14:16). The Holy Spirit is the one who is able to soothe our jittery nerves, and help us to relax. Sincerely from your heart you can pray and ask God believing to help you overcome the desire of cigarette smoking, and God will.

Secondly, drinking hinder the Spirit of God in the believer's life. Drinking gives us a false sense of courage. Drinking masks reality in the life of those who indulges excessively. Proverbs 20:1 says:

"Wine is a mocker, strong drink is raging: and whosoever is deceived thereby is not wise."

Also in Ephesians 5:18 it says:

"And be not drunk with wine, wherein is excess; but be filled with the Spirit."

Sincerely from your heart you can pray and ask God to deliver from wine and strong drink, and to fill you with the Holy Spirit, believing and God will.

Third, Fear will paralyze an individual. Fear causes us to not go forward. Know that your true source of courage comes

19

The Cycle of Sin

from the LORD. David in Psalms 27:14 says:

"I had fainted, unless I had believed to see the goodness of the LORD in the land of the living. Wait on the LORD: be of good courage, and he shall strengthen thine heart: wait, I say on the LORD."

Courage is the ability to face difficulty or danger with firmness, and without fear. Scripture tells us:

"For God hath not given us the spirit of fear, but of power, and of love, and of a sound mind (2 Timothy 1:7).*"*

Fourth, we are told in James 3:9-11, concerning cursing, that sweet and bitter water cannot flow out of the same fountain. Why then do some who are confessing Christ yet curse? And yes, there are those who do. We bless God in one breath, and speak cursing words in another, it should not be.

Fifth, adultery, fornication, and masturbation hinder the Spirit in the believer's life, and are three besetting sins. These besetting sins are with our bodies, which we are told that our bodies are the temple of the Holy Spirit, and they belong to God (1 Corinthians 6:19-20).

1 Corinthians 3:16-17 says:

"Know ye not that ye are the temple of God, and that the Spirit of God dwelleth in you? If any man defile the temple of God, him shall God (allow being) *destroy: for the temple of God is holy, which temple ye are."*

When we commit adultery, fornication, or masturbation, we are yielding our body to the flesh, and not to the Spirit of God. Sincerely from the heart pray and ask God believing to give you the power to yield your body as a living sacrifice, holy and acceptable which is your reasonable service and God will (Romans 12:1-2).

-2- The Cycle of Sin

Jesus in Matthew 11:28-30 says:

"Come unto me, all ye that labour and are heavy laden, and I will give you rest. Take my yoke upon you, and learn of me; for I am meek and lowly in heart: and ye shall find rest to your souls. For my yoke is easy, and my burden is light."

The word laden is the same word used in 2 Timothy 3:6 which speak of: *"silly women laden with sins, led away with diver lust:"*

There are so many who confess belief in Jesus, but fail to understand, that they must also learn of Him, for when they learn of who Jesus is, they learn who they are in Him. Jesus is God's only begotten Son. But, we are also sons and daughters of God, and God has made a way for us to come into His presence. It is called Worship, Praise, and Prayer.

However, sin weight heavy on our souls, but in Jesus we find rest (Hebrews 4:9-11). The rest that only comes when we come to Jesus, take His yoke upon us and learn of Him. Jesus is then able to lift every one of our heavy burdens and give us rest from our labor of sin. As I attempt to explain to the best of my ability this never ending cycle that can only be broken by the power of God through prayer and fasting or through the obedient act of your will.   I pray that you will see, perceive and or understand what all is involved in breaking from the cycle of sin!

The Cycle of Sin

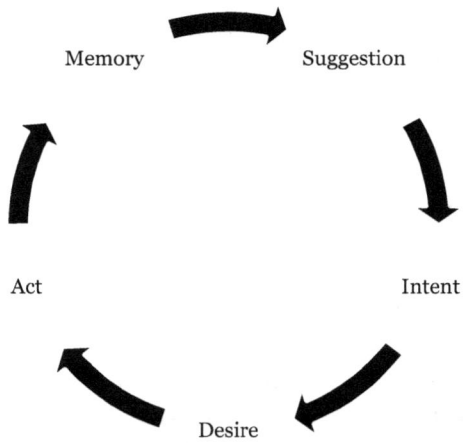

Memory → Suggestion → Intent → Desire → Act → Memory

___Chapter 3___

Suggestion

*"For God doth know that in the day ye eat thereof,
then your eyes shall be opened, and ye shall be as
gods, knowing good and evil."*
Genesis 3:5

Suggestion is the first link in the cycle of sin. Suggestion defined, is the act of suggesting; the process of inducing a thought, sensation or action in a receptive person, to mention, introduce or propose (an idea, or plan) for consideration, possible action or some purpose or use. Eve was the receptive person in the Garden of Eden and you and I are now, when we are tempted to sin. Before the fall of man, Adam was solely depended on God. But, when Adam and Eve disobeyed the personal commandment of God, not to eat from the tree of the knowledge of good and evil, they became independent of God and had the ability to choose good or evil. Adam and Eve after they had sin both eyes were opened and they realize that they were naked, and tried to cover their nakedness (or sin). The serpent who was in the person of the devil in the garden, twisted the truth by suggesting to Eve that she would not surely die. The lie that the serpent told Eve, that they would not surely die was the deception. They at that time did not experience physical death, but they did experience spiritual death. For this reason we must be born again of the Spirit of God to become the children of God (John 3:3-7).

When God created us, He blessed us to be fruitful and to multiply to replenish the earth. We were then told to have dominion over every living thing. For scripture says:

"So God create man in his own image, in the image of God created he him; male and female created he them. And God blessed them, and God said unto them. Be fruitful, and

23

multiply; and replenish the earth, and subdue it: and have dominion over the fish of the sea, and over the fowl of the air, and over every living thing that moveth upon the earth (Genesis 1:27-28)."

To reiterate, God created us to dominate every living thing. We have been given the capacity to emulate the character and attribute of God, who is our Creator, and is our heavenly Father. We have the capacity to express the same comfort, mercy, love, forgiveness, and compassion that God expresses toward us (2 Corinthians 1:3-4), and God has also given to us creativity.

Adam and Eve, was given a personal command not to eat from the tree of the knowledge of good and evil.

"And the serpent said unto the woman, Ye shall not surely die (Genesis 3:4)." Eve believed what was told her. The Bible says:

"And when the woman saw that the tree was good for food, and that it was pleasant to the eyes, and a tree to be desired to make one wise, she took of the fruit thereof, and did eat, and gave also unto her husband with her; and he did eat (Genesis 3:6)."

We see in motion the lust of the eyes, the lust of the flesh, and the pride of life, all of which are said to be in the world (1 John 2:16). Adam and Eve fell from their first estate, and a way had to be made for us to be restored, and given once again eternal life, and it was through Jesus Christ, our Lord and Savior. If Adam and Eve had not sinned or disobeyed the personal commandment of God, we would not have needed a Savior, and would not have been born into sin, spiritually dead (Ephesians 2:1).

Sin, presents itself first in a suggestion. For the sole purpose of clarity when the word suggestion is use replace it with the word temptation in your mind. Temptation, is nothing more than a suggestion to sin, a prompting to do something wrong. Again, sin first presents itself in a suggestion. When a suggestion is made, the individual must rely on the memory to make a choice as to whether he or she will enter into the next link which is intent.

Keep in mind, that the link of memory is part of the mind (heart). The mind houses the intellect, the emotions and the will.   The intellect is our thoughts or thinking process, which stores information we call knowledge. The emotions are our feelings, or emotional expressions which the mind stores in our memory past and present experiences. And the will is the part of the mind which carries out two functions, one of choice and two of action (or perseverance).   Again, the memory is the part of the mind which not only stores information, but our past and present experiences.

Prior to repentance, and our acceptance of Jesus Christ as our Savior, we were said to have been dead in our trespasses and sins, scripture says:

"And you hath he quickened, who were dead in trespasses and sins; Wherein in time past ye walked according to the course of this world, according to the prince of the power of the air (satan), *the spirit that now worketh in the children of disobedience: Among whom also we had our conversation* (conduct) *in times past in the lust of our flesh, fulfilling the desires of the flesh and of the mind; and was by nature the children of wrath, even as others* (sinners). *But God, who is rich in mercy, for his great love wherewith he loved us. Even when we were* (also) *dead in sins, hath quickened us together with Christ (by grace ye are saved☺:* (Ephesians 2:1-5). The word quicken, means made alive. We are made alive in Christ.

Now that we have been saved and made alive in Christ, speaking of believers who have been born of God's Spirit. We are now called to walk in the newness of life (Romans 6:1-7).

The Cycle of Sin

And, in order for us to walk in the newness of life, we must renew our minds. The Apostle Paul, in Romans 12:1-2, instructs us therefore to present our bodies as living sacrifices unto God, holy and acceptable which is our reasonably service. He tells us to no longer be conformed to this world, but to be transformed by the renewing of our minds so that we may prove that good, acceptable, and perfect Will of God. In other words, we are now called to yield our bodies to God, as living sacrifices, holy and acceptable, which is the least of our services. But, our conduct must change or be transformed by the renewing of our minds, so that we are no longer being conformed to this world.

Our minds are to be renewed through the Word of God. The Apostle Peter, because we have been born of God's Spirit tells us:

"Wherefore, laying (lay) *aside all malice, and all guile, and hypocrisies, and envies, and all evil speakings, As newborn babes, desire the sincere milk of the word, that ye may grow thereby: If so be ye have tasted that the Lord is gracious."*

When we refuse not to read or not study diligently the Word of God, the results are immature and carnal minded Christians. The local congregation will not reflect Jesus Christ, and the love needed to grow the Church spiritually will not be present (Ephesians 4:7-16).

When the Apostle Paul admonished us to lay aside every weight and the sin that so easily beset us and to let us run with patience the race which is before us, looking unto Jesus who is the author and finisher of our faith, we basically see two things. One, the need for us to no longer commit sin, and two, the need for us to grow. We grow by nourishing our spirit with the Word of God. We grow by obeying the Lord. Our growth depends on our willingness to obey the Lord (who is the Word of God).   In Matthew 4:4, Jesus says to the devil:

-3- Suggestion

"It is written, Man shall not live by bread alone, but by every word that proceedeth out of the mouth of God."

In reality, if we neglect eating physical food, the same way we do the reading, and the study of God's Word. We would be physically weak, and malnourished. Then we wonder why we cannot overcome the things that are in the world. It is because our spirits are weak, and malnourished.

When sin presents itself through a person's suggestion to you or even through your own thoughts caused by a trigger, simulate, or craving. The mind will process your thoughts by searching the memory, which will then locate past or present experiences concerning the suggestion. We call this recall. If the Word of God is not hid in your heart, to counteract your choice of entering into sin, you will yield to the flesh, and not the Spirit.

If the suggestion is extremely harmful, or has cause much sorrow. Your desire to please God rather than the flesh will cause you to not enter into the cycle of that particular sin (1 Peter 4:1-2). Often times, even if we have experienced extreme harm, or sorrow concerning a particular sin, which we call an addiction. The pleasure we first experience prior to the harm or sorrow will often time override our choice to not sin, and we end up giving in to the lust of our flesh.

Suggestion is the link to which you have the ability and the capacity to exercise your power of choice or free will. God did not take away our free will and we still have the ability or power to exercise it. For an individual whose mind have not been renewed through the Word of God, it is very difficult for him or her to resist the lust of the flesh. It is easier for them to give in, then to resist. James 4:7-8, gives us a way specifically, how we can break the cycle of sin. James says:

"Submit yourselves therefore to God. Resist (do not give into temptation) the devil, and he will flee from you.

The Cycle of Sin

The passage continues by saying:

"Draw nigh to God, and he will draw nigh to you. Cleanse your hands ye sinners, and purify your hearts ye double minded."

It is obvious to what this passage is saying, but I do want to bring to your attention who the Apostle James is speaking of concerning having a double mind. James is referring to the believer who is trying to live both within the world, and the kingdom of God (Luke 17:21; Romans 14:17). James says you are unstable in all your ways and your heart needs to be purified. How then do we purify our hearts? We purify our hearts by our hope in the Lord Jesus Christ, who is the hope of glory (Colossians 1:27). 1 John 3:1-3 says:

*"Behold, what manner of love the Father hath bestowed upon us that we should be called the sons of God: therefore the world knoweth us not, because it knew him not. Beloved, now are we the sons of God, and it doth not yet appear what we shall be: but we know that, when he shall appear, **we shall be like him**; for we shall see him as he is. And **every man that hath this hope** in him **purifieth himself**, even as **he is pure**."* This hope is we shall be like Him!

We either are walking according to the flesh, or according to the Spirit. There are no in between. The power behind your choice to live for Jesus Christ is your love for the Lord, and your knowledge and understanding of the Word of God, that it is true. What is hindering you? What is hindering you from obeying the Lord? What do you value more than your love for the Lord? These are questions we should ask ourselves. We must realize that a renewed mind is a mind that has been restored. We actually have to be taught again. We have to be taught how to live according to the ways of God. We have to learn how to love, how to forgive, how to trust, how to show mercy, how to show kindness, how to show compassion, and how to become content.

In my first book entitled, *Wisdom for Financial Success from a Biblical Perspective,* it teaches the principles of kingdom living and that our lives are not in monetary or material possessions. But that our lives are in Jesus Christ. Everything we need is in Christ. In Him we live, move and have our being (Acts 17:28). Jesus has provided us with many Great and Precious promises (2 Peter 1:4), and through faith we are to receive them. Truly knowing, understanding, and loving the Lord is what brings true contentment, which is very important in the believer's life. The Apostle Paul in Philippians 4:9-13 says:

"Those things, which ye have both learned, and received, and heard, and seen in me, do: and the God of peace shall be with you. But I rejoiced in the Lord greatly, that now at the last your care of me hath flourished again; wherein ye were also careful (caring), *but lacked opportunity. Not that I speak in respect of want: for I have learned, in whatsoever state I am, therewith to be content. I know both how to be abased, and I know how to abound: everywhere and in all things I am instructed both to be full and be hungry, both to abound and to suffer need. I can do all things through Christ which strengtheneth me."*

We have the power to overcome sin. The question we must ask ourselves is, am I going to continue walking in the lust of my flesh, or am I going to desire the things of God and become obedient to His Word? Sin in the believer's life, its affect and the result of us sinning will be the chastening of the Lord. God's Word shows us also that the soul that *sinneth it shall* (prematurely) *die* (Ezekiel 10:18-20). In 1 Corinthians 10:5-11 it says:

"But with many of them God was not well pleased; for they were overthrown in the wilderness. Now these things were our example, to the intent we should not lust after evil things, as they also lusted. Neither be ye idolaters, as were some of them; as it is written, The people sat down to eat and drink,

The Cycle of Sin

and rose up to play. Neither let us tempt Christ, as some of them also tempted, and were destroyed of serpents. Now all these things happened unto them for ensamples: and they are written for our admonition, upon whom the ends of the world are come:"

Sexual sin in the church is a big issue. We, speaking of the people of God, give in to adultery, fornication and masturbation because of sin that dwell in our flesh or mortal bodies. These three sins are very common in our churches today, and are the norm. We commit these three sins with no regard as to our bodies being the temple of the Holy Spirit. If God were to strike all who commit these sins (Ephesians 5:3) down as in the wilderness experience, half of our local congregations would perish. When we commit adultery, fornication and masturbation, we really are not giving consideration to what the Word of God is saying about our bodies being the temple of Holy Spirit. Or, do we just neglect finding out what is said, or rather we simply give in because of our desire to do our own will, rather than the will of God? Think about it.

When the suggestion to commit sin enters the mind, whether it is initiated by someone else or through your own thoughts, if the Word of God is not hidden in your heart to counteract the suggestion or temptation you will enter into the next link, which is intent. In this link you will determine your intention. What course of action you will take, whether you will give in to the lust of your flesh or to your desire to please and obey God. When the Word of God is hidden in your heart, which says for us to cast down imaginations and every high thing that exalt itself against the knowledge of God, and to bring into captivity every thought to the obedience of Christ, and your will act upon the Word spoken. The cycle will cease no matter which sin you are tempted to commit (2 Corinthians 10:4-6). I am not saying you will not struggle in making your choice. What I am saying is that your desire to please God must out weight the lust of your flesh. To resist means to not give in.

The more we resist the flesh in whatever sin we commit, the less hold it will have on us. Our love for the Lord must out weight the lust factor. If our minds could fully comprehend the death of Jesus Christ on the cross for our sins, we would not have any problem obeying the Lord. God know that we are mere human beings, so God made a way of escape for us. In I Corinthians 10:13 it says:

"There hath no temptation taken you but such as is common to man: but God is faithful, who will not suffer (allow) *you to be tempted above that ye are able; but will with the temptation also make a way to escape, that ye may be able to bear* (deal with) *it."*

Grace is God's enabling power given to the believer to overcome sin, and any given situation or circumstance we find ourselves facing. Grace is God's love, mercy and good will toward us undeserving. Grace is God's unmerited favor. There are so many ways we can prevent sinning if we really do not want to sin. Crucifying the flesh is agonizing, when we resist the flesh and do not give in to its lustful desires. But, obeying the Word of God is what gives us Victory. When it comes to sin we can leave the environment, better yet not go into it or right where we stand pray within our hearts seeking the Lord for guidance and direction. The Holy Spirit will speak to your heart, listen. These are all ways of escape.

Again, Jesus says in John 8:32: *"And ye shall know the truth, and the truth shall make you free."*

In this link, speaking of suggestion, the moment you do not give in to the temptation or suggest. You will cause the cycle of sin to cease. From this moment on you can intentionally obey the Lord, whenever you are tempted to sin by relying on the Holy Spirit to empower you, being prayerful and asking God to empower you. Should you willfully or intentionally give in to the temptation, repent, confess your sin asking God to forgive you, and then continue in obedience to the Lord!

The Cycle of Sin

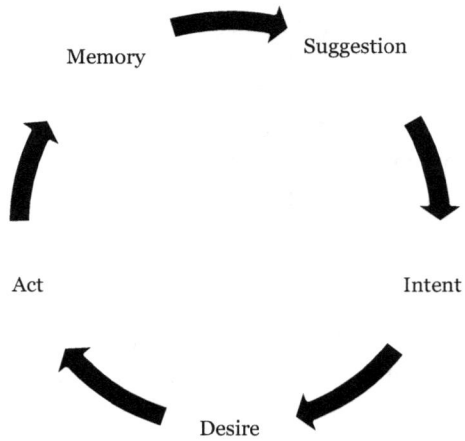

Memory → Suggestion

Suggestion → Intent

Intent → Desire

Desire → Act

Act → Memory

__Chapter 4__

Intent

*"The thief cometh not, but for to steal,
and to kill, and to destroy."*
John 10:10

Intent is the second link in the cycle of sin. The word Intent means something that is intended; an aim, purpose or design, and intended means to be deliberate or intentional. Intent is the link which gives us the opportunity to become real with God, the opportunity for us to no longer be hypocritical. Wearing masks and pretending to be godly, when we really are not. It gives us the opportunity to intentionally aim to obey the Lord, rather than to obey sin, or the lust of our flesh.

The thief (devil), come not but for to steal, and to kill, and to destroy. But, the intention of the Lord for us is to have life, and to have it more abundantly. The word abundantly means, occurring in or marked by abundance; plentiful, abounding with; rich. It is in Jesus Christ where we experience this abundance. Proverbs 10:22, confirms our abundance in the LORD, by letting us know that: *"The blessing of the LORD, it maketh rich, and **he addeth no sorrow with it** (Malachi 3:10).* Scripture also makes reference to us seeking worldly riches, and says: *But they that will* (desire to) *be rich fall into temptation and a snare, and into many foolish and harmful lusts, which drown men in destructions and perdition* (1 Timothy 6:9)." Why? *"For the love of money is the root of all evil: which while some coveted after, they have erred from the faith, and **pierced themselves through with many sorrows** (1 Timothy 6:10)."*

The Apostle Paul is speaking of the Church, how that the very desire to become rich will cause one to err from the faith, and that money is a snare which causes many to become

The Cycle of Sin

foolish, indulging in harmful lusts, that drown men in destructions and perdition (causes the loss of the soul).

Intention simply signifies a course of action that one proposes to follow. The intention of the Lord simply signifies a course of action that one proposes to follow, and in following the course of action being that of following Jesus. The Bible says: *"He* (or she) *shall receive the blessing from the LORD, and righteousness from the God of his* (her) *salvation* (Psalms 24:5).*"*

Whereas, the thief who is the devil, intentions are to steal, to kill, and to destroy. He targets your potential, hopes, and dreams, to deprive you of your life in Christ, and he intentionally attacks to destroy your joy and peace. The devil does so by causing you to live a foolish and sinful life. This is the intent of the devil. The devil as a roaring lion, walk about seeking whom he may devour, who we are told to resist steadfast in the faith knowing that those who are in the world are experiencing the same afflictions as we, yet do not have the Lord to whom they can cast their cares upon, for we know that He cares for us. We are also instructed to be sober and to be vigilant (watchful) 1 Peter 5:7-9. Because when we are not watchful (aware of the devices of the enemy), we will enter into sin through temptation, and giving in to temptation will cause us to remain in the cycle of sin. When we give in to sin, the devil takes us from our course to which we are commanded to follow, and we are once again walking according to the course of this world, which is a course of destruction.

Ephesians 2:1-2 says: *"And you hath he* (Jesus) *quickened who were dead in trespasses and sins. Wherein in time past ye walked according to the course of this world, according to the prince of the power of the air, the spirit that now worketh in the children of disobedience. Among whom also we all had our conversation* (conduct) *in time past, in the lust of our flesh, fulfilling the desires of the flesh and of the mind; and were by nature the children of wrath, even as others. But*

God, who is rich in mercy, for his great love wherein he loved us, Even when we were dead in sins, hath quickened us together with Christ, (by grace ye are saved;)" Now that we are saved, and have been born of the Spirit of God, the devil's aim is to take our attention away from God, and to place our focus on other things that are in the world such as the desire for pleasure, material possessions, popularity, fame and wealth. But, we are told that we are to humble ourselves under the mighty hands of God, and in due time, God will exalt us (1 Peter 5:6).

Humility is the way of life for the believer. But, the devil wants us to desire the things of the world, and to exalt ourselves. There is nothing wrong with having pleasure, as long as it is not sensuality. There is nothing wrong with having material possessions and being popular. There is nothing wrong with us becoming famous or wealthy. But if it takes us away from honoring, and serving God, then it is wrong.

These things, having pleasure, material possessions, popularity, fame, and wealth are baits the enemy dangle to entrap the people of God. The Apostle Paul says: *"But godliness with contentment is great gain. For we brought nothing into this world, and it is certain we can carry nothing out. And having food and raiment let us be therein content* (1 Timothy 6:6-8)." We cannot, speaking about the people of God, look at the world and what all they have, or how they come about to obtain it. But we must live, receive, and be blessed according to the Word of God.

Therefore, we are told in Psalms 37:1-2:

"Fret not thyself because of evildoers, neither be thou envious against the workers of iniquity. For they shall soon be cut down like the grass, and wither as the green herb."

If we look at what the world has, it may cause us to become

The Cycle of Sin

discontent. It may cause us to look at what we do not have rather than what we have already. It may cause us to become ungrateful, and if we are not careful. We will lack gratitude, and gratitude is part of our worship and praise.

The Bible tells us:

"In everything give thanks: for this is the will of God in Christ Jesus concerning you (1 Thessalonians 5:18)."

One way we can overcome the lusts of our flesh is by knowing the will of God for our lives. We are told in Matthew 6:33

"But seek ye first the kingdom of God, and his righteousness, and all these things shall be added unto you."

Jesus tells us to seek the things concerning God's Kingdom first and His righteousness, rather than us seeking to accumulate wealth, and or material possessions. We are prone to seeking those things which we see, rather than seeking the unseen. When in reality, it is the unseen things to which we need. When I speak of things unseen, I am talking about such things as wisdom, knowledge, understanding, power, and strength. These are the things we need to live a very successful Christian life.

Using common sense, we know if it is evil, it is not of God. But, God does use the wicked for the day of evil (Proverb 16:4). We know right from wrong, and the choices we made yesterday are the results of our today. This is the role disobedience play in our lives. When we disobey the Lord, we are not following the way that brings peace, joy, and contentment. The ways of the world, brings sorrow, despair, hopelessness and defeat. Jesus specifically tells us the right direction we are to follow.

"Jesus saith unto him, I am the way, the truth, and the life: no man cometh unto the Father, but by me (John 14:6)."

There are no other ways to God, and if we are not obeying the teachings of Jesus, then we are going in the wrong direction and not in the way of truth. Again, Jesus says:

. . . . ."*If ye continue in my word, then are ye my disciples indeed; And ye shall know the truth, and the truth shall make you free.*" John 8:31b-32   Freedom from the bondage of sin!

The Cycle of Sin

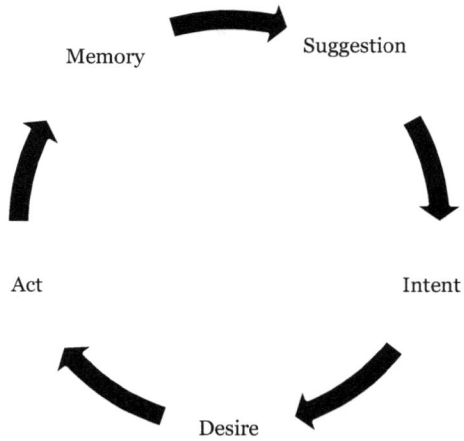

Memory → Suggestion → Intent → Desire → Act → Memory

__Chapter 5__

Desire

"But every man is tempted, when he is
Drawn away of his own lust, and enticed."
James 1:14

Desire is the third link in the cycle of sin. Desire is the opposite of lust. Desire defined is a longing or craving, as for something that brings satisfaction; hunger. Whereas, lust is an overwhelming desire or craving, both are similar in meaning. But unlike lust, desire causes one to move toward its object and is satisfied when it has attained its end. Lust on the other hand, is never satisfied, and takes you away from its object that being God. Desire is the link where choices are made and for the sole purpose of clarity, heart and mind are used interchangeably and are the same.

When I am speaking of the heart, I am talking about the mind. To bring clarity, Proverbs 23:7a says:

"For as he (a man) **thinketh** *in his heart* (mind), *so is he,* and in *Matthew 15:19-20a* it says:

"For out of the heart (mind**) *proceed evil thoughts,* *murders, adulteries, fornications, thefts, false witness,* *blasphemies: These are the things which defiles a man:"*

The Apostle Paul in 1 Thessalonians 5:23-24 says:

"And the very God of peace sanctify (separate) *you wholly;* *and I pray God your whole spirit and soul* (mind) *and body* *be preserved blameless unto the coming of our Lord Jesus* *Christ. Faithful is he that calleth you, who also will do it."*

Man is tribune, which means three parts, and consists of the

The Cycle of Sin

spirit, soul (mind), and the body. So in order for us to make the right choices, we must come to know and understand the functions of our minds, which is actually our hearts according to the Word of God. The mind (soul) or heart consists of the intellect, the emotions, and the will. Desire stems (or originate) from the soul (mind, or our innermost being), and lust from our flesh, or mortal bodies.

The mind houses the intellect, which is your thinking, the emotions, which are your feelings, and the will which governs your actions, or the choices you make. Choice is one function of the will, and the other is action, or perseverance. The will is governed by the intellect, and the emotions, and carry out their actions through the body. Therefore, the action of the will rely on what you think, and on how you feel, even though feelings do not play a role in obedience. Obedience is a command, and scripture does say for us to hate evil. Romans 12:9 NIV, refers to this by sayings:

"Love must be sincere. Hate what is evil; cling to what is good."

When you truly are saved, sanctified, and filled with the Holy Ghost. You will have no notion (an inclination) of sinning, yet you will be tempted. When you are hypocritical and sin presents itself in a suggestion. Your desire whether it is to please God or your flesh will rely on your memory to make the necessary choice, as to whether you are going to obey God, or your flesh.

Unless, you have the Word of God hidden in your heart, and act upon it to counteract what you are being tempted of, you will give in to the lust of your flesh. Keep in mind that the memory not only hides God's Word. But, it also has past and present feelings, and experiences it relies on to make its choice or decisions. All this is happening sub-consciously.

One critical area the devil hinders us in our spiritual

40

growth, is when we give in to adultery, fornication and uncleanness. These three betting sins are with our bodies, which are the temples of the Holy Spirit. Even though we are aware of our choice to sin, our desire to not sin is not backed up with knowing and understanding the Word of God. When God's Word is not hidden in our heart for our will to act upon it, we will sin. We sin because we really do not understand the consequences of our actions. When we really believe we should not commit adultery, fornication or masturbation (Ephesians 5:3). We will not commit adultery, fornication or masturbation. In our minds somewhere we are rationalizing our need to commit these sins. We have to deal with these three sins, because they keep us in bondage. We rationalize, because we feel God understands that we are human, and God has given us the sex drive. Yes, God did give us the sex drive, but He also has established marriage for this very reason, along with us to be fruitful, and to multiply. We may very well want to obey God, but scripture says that our spirit is willing, but our flesh is weak. So, Jesus tells His disciples in Matthew 26:41 to:

"Watch and pray, that ye enter not into temptation: the spirit indeed is willing, but the flesh is weak."

We will be tempted, but being aware, discerning, and watchful, along with praying to ask God for strength and power are all ways of preventing us from entering into the cycle of sin.

Understand that the spirit of man is the part of man which connects with the immaterial, spiritual realm, or God. It is the intuitive or intuition, and communion. The body of man is the part of man which connects with the material or physical realm, or the physical world. So you must nourish your spirit man which is your born-again nature created after God, by feeding it through the Word of God, so as to help you to grow stronger in the spirit, as you hide or memorize the Word in your heart, or mind. The will sub-consciously act upon the Word of God which is hidden in your heart (mind), as you

41

desire to live a holy and righteous life. Say your desire is not to live a holy and righteous life. Guess what? You will not live a holy and righteous life. You will remain in your lustful ways.

The sole purpose of renewing your mind is so that your will which is housed in your mind, may act upon the Word of God hidden in your heart, rather than what you are thinking or how you are feeling. The Apostle Paul in Romans 12:1-2, says:

I beseech you therefore, brethren, by the mercies of God, that ye present your bodies a living sacrifice, holy, acceptable unto God, which is your reasonable service. And be not (no longer) *conformed to this world, but be ye transformed by the renewing of your mind that ye may prove what is that good and acceptable, and perfect, will of God."*

We prove the Word of God is true by bringing it about in our lives through obedience.

When your will rely on what you are thinking, and on how you are feeling, it is said that you are walking in the flesh, or according to the flesh. When your will rely on the intellect that has been renewed by hiding or memorizing the Word of God in your mind or heart and your will acts upon it. You are said to be in obedience, and are walking in the spirit, or according to the Spirit of God. So then, understanding that desire initiates growth, and lust hinders it, will help you to intentionally focus your attention on growing stronger in the Lord.

Your goal now then would be to renew your mind by memorizing the Word of God, so that your will act upon the God's Word which is hidden in your heart, rather than on what you are thinking, or feeling, as you desire to live a holy and righteous life. When this happens, you are said to becoming spiritually mature. Your desire should then be to grow stronger in the Lord, by the renewing of your mind continually. Think of it this way, you will have to learn everything you know again, but according to the ways of God.

What does the Bible say about the flesh, and the Spirit? The Bible lets us know that they are in conflict with one another.

"This I say then, Walk in the Spirit (or according to the Word of God)*, and ye shall not fulfill the lust of the flesh. For the flesh lusteth against the Spirit, and the Spirit against the flesh: and these are contrary the one to the other: so that ye cannot do the things that ye would* (Galatians 5:16-17).*"*

The Apostle Paul explains here that both the flesh and the Spirit of God want control of your life. When you give the flesh control, then you are not able to do according to the will of God, and when you give the Spirit of God control, you are not able to do according to the lust of the flesh. You have the power to make either choice, but the question is? Where is your heart? Is your heart for the things of God or for the things of this world?   So, the Apostle Paul says, walk in the Spirit, and you will not fulfill the lust of the flesh.

Jesus in Matthew 6:24, tells us also that:

"No man can serve two masters: for either he will hate the one, and love the other; or else he will hold to the one, and despise (reject) *the other. Ye cannot serve God and mammon."* Mammon is the personification of wealth or riches, and is the god of this present world (2 Corinthians 4:4).

John 8:34, goes on to say:

"Jesus answered them (those Jews who believed not)*, Verily, verily I say unto you, Whosoever committeth sin is a servant of sin. And the servant* (of sin) *abideth not in the house for ever; but the Son abideth ever. If the Son therefore shall make you free, ye shall be free indeed."*

Jesus is the only one who can empower us to become free from the power of sin in our lives, and He does so by the truth of God's Word. You and I both would remain in our sin without the truth. This is why we are told by the Apostle James, to be not only hearers, but doers of the Word (James 1:22).

Jesus gives us this promise in Matthew 5:6: **"blessed are they which do hunger (desire) and thirst after righteousness: for they shall be filled."** His promise is to those who hunger and thirst after the Righteousness of God, shall be filled with the Holy Spirit, who will then enable or empower you to live for God. Many find it very hard to surrender their will, to the will of God. Why? Because they do not fully understand what it means to Surrender. Surrender, means to give up absolutely everything. To give up your vices, desires, ambition, plans, and goals while seeking God's will, guidance, and directions. Doing what you know is right, while allowing God to reveal or to unfold to your understanding His will for your life. When we surrender our will, to the will of God, we give the Holy Spirit permission to empower or to enable us to live a holy and righteous life.

In Psalms 37:3-9, we are told by David to: *"Trust in the LORD, and do good; so shalt thou dwell in the land, and verily thou shalt be fed. Delight thyself* (take pleasure) *also in the LORD; and he shall give thee the desires of thine heart* (the LORD will literally place his desires for your life in your heart). *Commit* (hand over) *thy way unto the LORD; trust also in him; and he shall bring it* (his desires for your life) *to pass. And he shall bring forth thy righteousness as the light, and thy judgment as the noonday. Rest in the LORD, and wait **patiently** for him: fret not thyself because of him who prospereth in his way, because of the man who bringeth wicked devices to pass. Cease from anger, and forsake wrath: fret not thyself in any wise to do evil. For evildoers shall be cut off: but those that **wait upon the LORD**, they shall inherit the earth* (for eternity).*"*

Notice that everything the LORD promises, He is the one who brings it to pass. He brings your righteousness and judgment to pass! Righteousness is being in right standing with God, acting in accord with divine or moral law and judgment is the ability to make good decisions about what should be done. To clarify that the Lord places His desires in our hearts, we can go to Psalms 78:29-32, and it says:

"So they did eat, and were well filled: for he (the Lord) ***gave them their own desire****: They were not estranged from their lust. But while their meat was yet in their mouths, The wrath of God came upon them, and slew the fattest of them, and smote down the chosen men of Israel. For all this they sinned still, and believed not for his wondrous works."*

This is the account of the children of Israel in the wilderness. Even though God gave them water from a rock, and rain manna from heaven, scripture says, *"And they tempted God in their heart by asking meat **from their lust*** (Psalms 78:18)."* In other words, they were dissatisfied with the will of God, and God gave them meat to which **they desired**, as when they were in Egypt. When you no longer desire the things of the world, and begin to **desire the things of God**, you will experience change. It is called conversion!

The Cycle of Sin

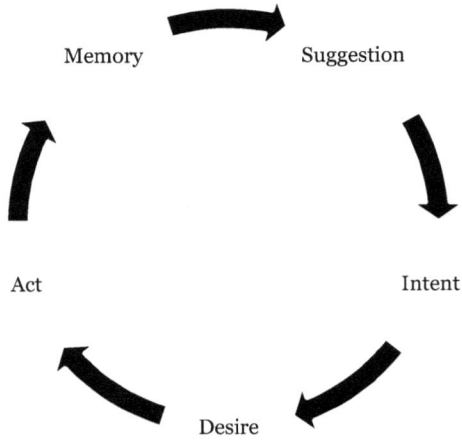

Memory → Suggestion

Suggestion → Intent

Intent → Desire

Desire → Act

Act → Memory

__Chapter 6__

Act

"When a man's ways please the LORD,
he maketh even his enemies to be at peace with him."
Proverbs 16:7

Act is the fourth link in the cycle of sin. Act defined is the process of doing or performing something. Act simply means to do. Act is the link which we are called upon to do what we say we believe. If we say we believe that the Word of God is true, then how come we are not doing it?   Could it be that our minds which are our hearts, do not fully understand the Word of God? Could we be depended solely on our emotions, rather than relying on the Word of God? We hear the Word of God, it excites us, but yet we do not have the power to say no to our sinful flesh, which lust after its own desires. In James 2:19, it says:

"Thou believest that there is one God; thou do well: the devils also believe and tremble. But wilt thou know, O vain man, that faith without works is dead?"

Belief is one thing, and obedience is another thing. When we believe only, it is what James calls dead faith. The Apostle James illustrates to us what faith without works is, when he compare it to the body without the spirit and says:

"For as the body without the spirit is dead, so faith without works (acting on what we say we believe) *is dead also."*

There are those of us, speaking about the people of God, who say they believe that the Word of God is true. But, fail to act upon it, simply because they do not know or fully understand how the will operates. The will relies on the memory to carry out the action of its choice, or choices. Have you heard the

47

saying garage in garage out? What is in your heart will come out. We hide behind our masks, when we are around one another, but when we are away from the saints. We remove our masks and stop pretending to live godly lives. We let our guards down, and resume the drinking, smoking, cursing, gossiping, backbiting, fornication, uncleanness, and the everything else. It is time for us, the people of God to empty our minds of garage. What is in your heart will surely come out sooner or later. Soon then later deception will show its ugly head. The Apostle James makes a point that those who are only hearers of the Word are deceiving their own selves. He instructs us by saying:

"Wherefore lay apart all filthiness and superfluity of naughtiness, and receive with meekness the engrafted word, which is able to save your souls. But be ye doers of the word, and not hearers only, deceiving your own selves (James 1:21-22)."

It is time for the people of God to cleanse their hearts. It is time for the people of God to empty their minds of garage. It is time for the people of God to rid or empty their minds of the things of this world. It is time for the people of God, to renew their minds with the Word of God. Then and only then will we be able to live according to the ways of God. Jesus says:

"A good man out of the good treasure of the heart bringeth forth good things: and an evil man out of the evil treasure bringeth forth evil things (Matthew 12:35)."

Proverbs 16:7 says, *"When a man's ways please the LORD, he maketh even his enemies to be at peace with him."* Are you being tormented by the devil's unclean, wicked, foul, and evil spirits? Are you being provoked to anger? Is the enemy hindering your pursue of God? Take a close look at life how you are living. Are you living according to the revealed will of God? Better yet, do you even desire to obey God? If we are to please God, we must act upon what we say we believe, understanding that faith without works is dead.   Hebrews 11:6, says:

"But without faith it is impossible to please him: for he that cometh to God must believe that he is, and that he is a rewarder of them that diligently seek him."

So then, how do we diligently seek God, that we may please Him?   First of all, we should acknowledge God when He awakens us in the morning.   We should then acknowledge the LORD, thanking God for allowing us to see another day.   For the Psalmist says: *"This is the day which the LORD hath made; we will rejoice and be glad in it* (Psalms 118:24)*."* Once we realize, that the LORD God did not have to wake us up and that there were many, who did not awake. We will develop a heart of gratitude.

One reason we do not seek God as we should, is because we do not want to put forth the effort it takes to seek the LORD. Secondly, we do not want to be told by anyone what you should do. Third, could it be that we really do not see a need to seek God, as we should or maybe we just do not understand how we are to seek the LORD?

The word diligently means to put forth painstaking effort, and the word seek, means to go to, or toward; to try to discover, as by studying; to go in search, or quest of.   Isaiah 55:6-8 tells us to:

"Seek ye the LORD while he may be found, call upon him while he is near: Let the wicked (unsaved) *forsake his way, and the unrighteous man* (saved) *his thoughts: and let him return unto the LORD, and he will have mercy upon him; and to our God, for he will abundantly pardon."*

Isaiah first of all, lets us know that there will come a time when the LORD will not be found, and we will call upon Him, and not be heard, in that He will not answer us. Isaiah goes on to make a distinction between the wicked, and the unrighteous man. The wicked man is going the way of wickedness, and is told to forsake his way. But, the unrighteous man is told to forsake his **thoughts**. Why? What is Isaiah saying about the unrighteous man? The Prophet Isaiah is saying that the unrighteous man was once righteous, but allowed his thinking to cause him to become unrighteous (backslidden). When these two individuals return unto the LORD, He will have mercy on the wicked man, and the unrighteous man, He will forgive, and they both are to not only return unto the LORD, but to God.

Next, we should begin our day with prayer. Be specific, and ask God for what you need. Father give me strength, grace, and mercy! Pray His blessing also upon others and ask God to help them. Along with prayer, you must set aside time to read, and for those of us who know how to study, to study the Word of God. How do we then determine the best time to set this time apart? Listen to what David says in Psalms 63:1-7:

*"O GOD, thou art my God; **early will I seek thee:** my soul thirsteth for thee, my flesh longeth for thee in a dry and thirsty land, where no water is; To see thy power and thy glory, so as I have seen thee in the sanctuary. Because thy lovingkindness is better than life, my lips shall praise thee. Thus will I bless thee while I live: I will lift up my hands in thy name. My soul shall be satisfied as with marrow and fatness; and my mouth shall praise thee with joyful lips: **When I remember thee upon my bed, and meditate on thee in the night watches.** Because thou hast been my help, therefore in the shadow of thy wings will I rejoice."*

David not only sought God early, but at night he is said to have remembered Him, while upon his bed in the night watches. Whether you read, or study the Word of God, at any given time. Pray first, and ask God to enlighten your eyes of understanding, and to give unto you the spirit of wisdom, and revelation of the knowledge of His Son, Jesus Christ. God will help you to understand, and apply His Word to your life. If possible, pray the same time each day you come before God . When you begin to read, and study the Word of God. You will then develop an appetite which will cause you to want more of God's Word. So then, what does the Word say about us renewing our mind? We are told to study:

"Study to show thyself approved unto God, a workman that needeth not to be ashamed, rightly dividing the word of truth (2 Timothy 2:15)."

Study is much more than reading the Bible. It is giving yourself over to learning. It is taking the Word of God and dividing it into small sections, learning a little here, and a little there. Actually, this is how we learn. The Prophet says in Isaiah 28:9-10:

"Whom shall he (God) *teach knowledge? And whom shall he make to understand doctrine* (teaching)? *them that are weaned from the milk, and drawn from the breasts. For precept must be upon precept, precept upon precept; line upon line, line upon line; here a little, and there a little.*

So many, of the people of God, know the Word, yet do not have the power to say no, to the flesh. Those who know the Word of God, but fail to implement it in their lives are said to be unskillful in the Word of righteousness meaning, they have need that one teach them again which be the first principles of the oracles of God (Hebrews 6:1-6).

In Hebrews 5:12-14, we are told: *"For when for the time ye ought to be teachers, ye have need that one teach you again which be the first principles of the oracles of God; and are become such as have need of milk, and not of strong meat. For every one that useth milk is unskillful in the word of righteousness: for he is a babe. But strong meat belongeth to them that are of full age, even those who by reason of use have their senses exercised to discern both good and evil.*

The Cycle of Sin

The Apostle Peter goes on and says:

"As newborn babes, desire the sincere milk of the word, that ye may grow thereby."

Desire is very important, when it comes to the reading and studying of God's Word. Desire is what initiates growth, and lust is what hinders it. Proverbs 13:12b-13 says:

"but when desire cometh, it is a tree of life. Whoso despiseth (reject) *the word shall be destroyed: but he that feareth the commandment shall be rewarded."*

God is not only a rewarder of them that diligently seek Him. But, He will make even your enemies to be at peace with you, when your ways please the LORD. To sum this up:

"As for God, his way is perfect; the word of the LORD is tried (proved): *he is a buckler* (shield) *to all them that trust in him. For who is God, save the LORD? And who is a rock, save our God. God is my strength and power; and he maketh my way perfect (2 Samuel 22:31-33)."* *"Be ye therefore perfect, even as your Father which is in heaven is perfect* (Matthew 5:44-48)".

__Chapter 7__

Memory

"forgetting those things which are behind, And reaching forth unto those things which are before.
Philippians 3:13c

Memory is the fifth link in the cycle of sin. Memory defined is, the mental faculty of retaining and recalling past and present experiences; the ability of the mind to store and recall past and present sensations, thoughts, knowledge; the sum of everything retained by the mind. Memory is the link which processes our choice, or the decisions that we make. Memory is the link to which the will rely on to carry out its actions.

The Apostle Paul speaking in the above scripture is giving instructions for us to forget our past.   First of all, Why? 2 Corinthians 5:17 -19, says:

"Therefore if any man be in Christ, he is a new (creation) *creature: old things are passed away; behold, all things are become new. And all things are of God, who hath reconciled us to himself by Jesus Christ, and hath given us **the ministry of reconciliation**: To wit, that God was in Christ reconciling the world unto himself, not imputing their trespasses unto them; and hath committed unto us the word of reconciliation."*

We have now become instruments of God's Righteousness, instruments that are to be use of God to lead others to Christ. An instrument cannot play itself. Therefore, it is God who does the work through us.   The Apostle Paul is saying that we are now ambassadors for Christ, and we who have been reconciled to God, now has the ministry of reconciling others to God through Christ Jesus. (2 Corinthians 5:20). We are called to no longer miss the mark. But, are now call to

53

press toward the mark for the prize of the high calling of God which is in Christ Jesus. The Apostle Paul says that we are to forget those things which are behind, and to take hold of our new life in Jesus Christ. Jesus has called us to walk in the newness of life. We are called to forget our past experiences, and to take hold of our new life in Jesus Christ. I repeated that twice intentionally. We need to know and understand that we have been born again of the Spirit of God, and are now accepted in the beloved (1 John 3:2). Our life is now in Jesus Christ.

The Apostle Paul speaking of his old background says in Philippians 3:2-7:

"Beware of dogs, beware of evil workers, beware of the concision. For we are the circumcision, which worship God in the spirit, and rejoice in Christ Jesus, and have no confidence in the flesh. Though I might also have confidence in the flesh. If any other man thinketh that he hath whereof he might trust in the flesh, I more. Circumcised the eighth day, of the stock of Israel, of the tribe of Benjamin, an Hebrew of the Hebrews; as touching the law, a Pharisee; Concerning zeal, persecuting the church; touching the righteousness which is in the law, blameless. But what things were gain to me, those I counted loss for Christ."

Paul continues on in Philippians 3:13c-14 by saying:

"forgetting those things which are behind, And reaching forth unto those things which are before. I press toward the mark for the prize of the high calling of God in Christ Jesus."

He explains in next passage of scriptures for us to:

"Be careful (anxious) for nothing; but in everything by prayer and supplication with thanksgiving let your request be made known unto God. And the peace of God, which passeth all understanding shall keep (guard) your hearts and

minds through Christ Jesus (Philippians 4:6-7)." Heart in this context denotes (the innermost being or emotions).

Paulexplains that we are to bring all our concerns to God, and then He says in Philippians 4:8-9:

*"Finally, brethren, whatsoever things are true, whatsoever things are honest, whatsoever things are just, whatsoever things are pure, whatsoever things are lovely, whatsoever things are of good report; if there be any virtue, and if there be any praise, **think on these things**. Those things, which ye have both learned, and received, and heard, and seen in me, do: and the God of peace shall be with you."*

What in fact the Apostle Paul is saying is that, we need not focus our minds on not having or needing anything. We are to trust the Lord (Proverbs 3:5-6). We do so by prayer and supplication, letting our requests be made known to God, knowing that God hears and answers prayers according to His will. We can rest or wait on God, knowing that He is faithful, and true that He will keep us in perfect peace whose mind is stay on Him. The Apostle John encourages us also by saying:

"These things have I written unto you that believe on the name of the Son of God, that ye may know that ye have eternal life, and that ye may believe on the name of the Son of God. And this is the confidence that we have in him, that if we ask any thing according to his will, he heareth us: And if we know that he hear us, whatsoever we ask, we know that we have the petitions (requests) *that we desired* (have asked) *of him (* 1 John 5:13-15)."*

We are not to focus our attention on those things which we have need of or on any negativity (Matthew 6:33). We need not allow our past feelings, or experiences to remain or to re-surface in our minds (hearts). We are to give our total attention to the things of God and place our focus on the things which are positive. Positive thinking originated from the Word of God. Positive thinking originated from the passage of scripture in Philippians 4:8-9.

Now that we are in Jesus Christ, we can no longer allow the devil to bring back to our remembrance our past sins. When we confess our sins, and ask God to forgive us. The Bible says that God cast our sins into the sea of forgetfulness to remember them no more.

The Prophet Micah asks this question:

"Who is a God like unto thee, that pardoneth iniquity; and passeth by the transgression of the remnant of his heritage? He retaineth not his anger for ever, because he delighteth in mercy. He will turn again, he will have compassion upon us; he will subdue our iniquities; and thou wilt cast all their sins into the depths of the sea. Thou wilt perform the truth to Jacob, and the mercy to Abraham, which thou hast sworn unto our fathers from the days of old (Micah 7:18-20)."

Guess what? We are the seed of Abraham, and the blessing of Abraham is upon us! (Genesis 12:3; Genesis 28:1-4)

Memory is the link, where we are to make new, to start over, to replace the content of our minds with the Word of God. Why? Because thoughts are substance and before substance can be manifested there must be thought. Thought is spirit, the unseen. But, it does not remain unseen. The thoughts of man are soon revealed in the substance of his deeds, which follow those thoughts. The Bible says it like this:

"Now faith is the substances (thoughts) of things hoped for, the evidence of things not seen."

Even though what we believe (faith) is not seen. Its presence is in our minds (hearts), and our hearts can see what we believe, before it is manifested. Romans 10:6-10, says:

"But the righteousness which is of faith speaketh on this wise, Say not in thine heart, Who shall ascend into heaven? (that is, to bring Christ down from above.) Or, Who shall descend unto the deep? (that is, to bring Christ again from the dead.) But what saith it? The word is nigh thee, even in thy mouth, and in thy heart; that is, the word of faith, which we preach: That if thou shalt confess with thy mouth the Lord Jesus, and shalt believe in thine heart that God hath raised him from the dead, thou shalt be saved. For with the heart man believeth unto righteousness. And with the mouth confession is made unto salvation."

Those who believe they have not been saved through their confession of the Lord Jesus Christ, are still living unsaved lives, because they fail to understand that they must renew their minds and become obedient to the Lord. Therefore, they do not know that when they do sin, they can ask forgiveness and God will forgive them. But, when we sin intentionally or willfully after we have confessed Christ, we have not truly repented. 1 John 1:6-8 tells us:

"If we say that we have fellowship with him, and walk in darkness (ignorance or sin), *we lie, and do not the truth. But if we walk in the light* (truth), *as he is in the light, we have fellowship one with another, and the blood of Jesus Christ his Son cleanseth us from all sin. If we say that we have no sin, we deceive ourselves, and the truth is not in us."*

The next two verses are very important for us to understand. John the Apostle continues by saying:

"If we confess our sins, he is faithful and just to forgive us our sins, and to **cleanse us from all unrighteousness**. *If we say that we have not sinned, we make him a liar, and his word is not in us* (1 John 1:9-10)."*

When you confess your sins to God, it means that you admit you have done wrong. Now imagine confessing every time you commit sin intentionally or willfully. You would sound like abroken record. This is why you do not find many people who are actually confessing their sins to God. They just sin, and when their conscience began to wear on them, then they are sorry and confess, but it is not godly sorrow. Godly sorrow causes us to repent, confess our sins, and desire to not sin. When you truly repent, you turn from your sin and dedicate your life to God doing everything necessary to not sin intentionally. Your behavior will change. But, in order for your behavior to change you must change the way you think.

Apostle Paul in Philippians 2:5-8, gives us insight also into steps which will help us become obedient to God. He says:

"Let this mind be in you which was also in Christ Jesus: Who, being in the form of God, thought it not robbery to be equal with God: But, made himself of no reputation, and took upon him the form of a servant, and was made in the likeness of men: And being found in fashion as a man, he humbled himself, and became obedient unto death, even the death of the cross."

Jesus, being in the form of God, was made in the likeness of men, and being found in fashion as a man, we are told that He made Himself of no reputation, took upon Himself the form of a servant, humbled Himself and became obedient unto God, even unto the death of the cross. Scripture even says in Hebrews 5:8-9, *"Though he were a Son, yet learned obedience by the things which he suffered; And being made perfect, he became the author* of eternal salvation unto all ***them that obey him.***"

We too must make ourselves of no reputation, become servants, humble ourselves and obey the Lord on purpose. Jesus did not die on the cross for us to continue in our sin. He died to restore us to our rightful place in God, so that we would have a right to the tree of life and live eternally with God. We are called to take our cross up daily, to follow

Jesus through obedience (Luke 9:23), while crucifying the deeds of our flesh by putting our flesh to death (not giving in).

While Memory is the link, which we must empty our minds of garage, and make new, start over and replace it with the Word of God. Memory is the link also that we must not allow our past to cause us to not go forth in Jesus Christ. Memory is the link where we must come to understand and know that we are the Righteousness of God, and must now walk in our righteousness which is by faith in the Lord, Jesus Christ.

 In Romans 3:22-26 it says:

 "But now the righteousness of God without the law (of sin) *is manifested, being witnessed by the law* (of God) *and the prophets; even the righteousness of God which is by faith of Jesus Christ unto all and upon all them that believe: for there is no difference: For all have sinned, and come short of the glory of God; Being justified freely by his grace through the redemption that is in Christ Jesus; Whom God hath set forth to be a propitiation* (an atoning sacrifice) *through faith in his blood, to declare his righteousness for the remission of sins that are past, through the forbearance of God; To declare, I say, at this time his righteousness: that he might be just, and the justifier of him which believeth in Jesus."*

When we change our mind, we change our behavior. It is called the renewing of the mind (Romans 12:1-2). What we say and do are two different stories. If we say we believe God, then why do our actions say otherwise? We must become obedient, and in doing so. We have Victory over sin. A quote from an unknown source says, "Your belief does not make you a better person, your behavior does!

The Cycle of Sin

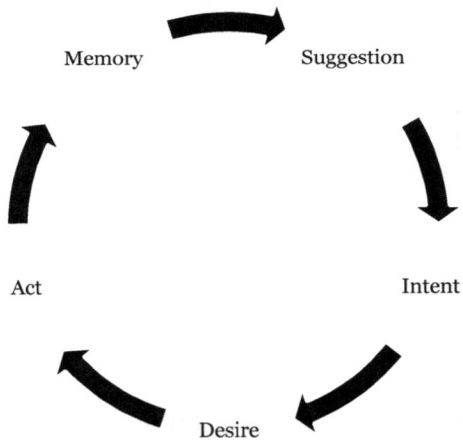

Memory → Suggestion → Intent → Desire → Act → Memory

__Chapter 8__

Victory over Sin

"THERE is therefore now no condemnation to them which are in Christ Jesus. Who walk not after the flesh, but after the Spirit."
Romans 8:1

The Apostle Paul in Romans 8:2 reveals the solution to overcoming sin in our lives. He says:

For the law of the Spirit of life in Christ Jesus hath made me free from the law of sin and death."

Paul makes known that there are two laws operating in the believer's life. The sinner naturally sin, and the law of sin and death is operating in his or her life. But because we have been born of God's Spirit, we either can walk in the flesh, or the spirit. The choice is ours. We no longer have one nature, but two. These two natures are the old man and the new man, which after God is created in righteousness and true holiness. In Ephesians 4:20-23, the Apostle Paul says:

"But ye have not so learned Christ; If so be that ye have heard him, and have been taught by him, as the truth is in Jesus: That ye put off concerning the former conversation (conduct of) *the old man, which is corrupt according to the deceitful lusts; And be renewed in the spirit of your mind; And that ye put on the new man, which after God is created in righteousness and true holiness."*

Whichever law you allow to operate in your life, is the law that will dictate your life. When you allow the law of sin and death to operate in your life, the old man, or nature is in control. If you allow the law of the Spirit of Life in Christ Jesus to operate in your life, the new man or nature is in control. When you continue to walk in darkness or sin, the law of sin and death is operating in your life, and is in control. Truth be told, you are living a defeated life. **Victory over sin is obedience** through faith in the Lord, Jesus Christ.

In revealing the cycle of sin, the Apostle Paul says:

*"for the good that I would I do not: but the evil which I would not, that I do. Now if I do that I would not, it is no more I that do it, **but sin that dwelleth in me**. I thank God through Jesus Christ our Lord. So then with the mind I myself serve the law of God; but with the flesh the law of* sin (Romans 7:19-20, 25).*"*

God has given us free will. We have a choice as to whether we are going to sin, or become obedience to the Word of God. The Apostle Paul is saying in these verses that you have the power to choose which law you will allow to operate in your life. You can either serve the law of God, which is the law of the Spirit of life in Christ Jesus, as you renew your mind or you can continue to serve the law of sin and death by walking after the lust of your flesh. When you choose to walk after the lust of your flesh and not after the Spirit of God, you will experience the ill-effect of sin, which is condemnation.

Condemnation is the state of being condemn, and condemn means to cause (someone) to suffer or live in difficult or unpleasant conditions. The Apostle Paul understood this when he warned us against the partaking of the Lord's Supper unworthily. He says in Hebrew 10:26, for those who do, they trodden underfoot the Son of God, and count the blood of the covenant, an unholy thing. When we constantly sin, we can fall from grace into the hands of the living God!

The Apostle Paul says:

"for he that eateth and drinketh unworthily, eateth and drinketh damnation to himself, not discerning the Lord's

body. For this cause (or reason) *many are weak and sickly among you, and many sleep* (are dead). *For if we would judge ourselves, we should not be judged. But when we are judged, we are chastened of the Lord, that we should not be condemned with the world* (1 Corinthians 11:26-32).

We have been called to walk worthy of the Lord. The Apostle Paul spoke these words to the Colossian Church:

"For this cause we also since the day we heard (of your faith) *it. Do not cease to pray for you, and to desire that ye might be filled with the knowledge of his will in all wisdom and spiritual understanding: That ye might walk worthy of the Lord unto all pleasing, being fruitful in every good work, and increasing in the knowledge of God; Strengthened with all might, according to his glorious power, unto all patience and longsuffering with joyfulness; Giving thanks unto the Father, which hath made us meet (qualified) to be partakers of the inheritance of the saints in light: Who hath (God) delivered us from the power of darkness, and hath translated us into the kingdom of his dear Son: In whom we have redemption through his blood, even the forgiveness of sins:* (Colossians 1:9-14)."*

We who are saved have already been delivered from the power of darkness, and are translated into the kingdom of God. We must now seek to understand what all have been provided for us, now that we are in the kingdom, and have been saved. We must now walk in our deliverance. We walk in our deliverance by faith and not by sight. We cannot go by what we see, feel, or think. We must stand on the Word of God. The word stand means, to remain in an upright position. We must walk in obedience to the Lord Jesus Christ unto all pleasing (Proverbs 10:9; Proverbs 14:2).

Your desire to obey the LORD, must out weight the lust of your flesh, and in order to out weight the lust of your flesh, you must have knowledge of the truth, because the truth is what makes us free from the bondage of sin, and death. The law of sin and death is what keeps us in bondage to sin. So the Apostle Paul in Galatians 5:1 says:

"Stand fast therefore in the liberty (freedom) *wherewith Christ hath made us free, and be not entangled again with the yoke of bondage."*

The Apostle Paul also tells us in Galatians 5:16-18:

"This I say then, Walk in the Spirit, and ye shall not fulfill the lust of the flesh. For the flesh lusteth against the Spirit, and the Spirit against the flesh: and these are contrary the one to the other: so that ye cannot do the things that ye would. But if ye be led of the Spirit, ye are not under the law (law of sin and death).*"*

Again, the flesh and the Spirit of God want control of your life. When you give the flesh control, then you are not able to do according to the will of God, and when you give the Spirit of God control, you are not able to do according to the lust of the flesh. You have the power to choose which law you want to operate in your life. You must choose to obey the commandments of Jesus Christ, by implementing each precept in your life, which will give you victory over sin. Your growth depends on your willingness to obey God. How then does the process begin?

"And be renewed in the spirit of your mind; And that ye put on the new man, which after God is created in righteousness and true holiness (Ephesians 4:23-24.*"*

Jesus lets us know also in John 6:63:

"It is the spirit that quickeneth; the flesh profiteth nothing: the words that I speak unto you, they are spirit, and they are life."

Jesus is saying that our spirit has been made alive in Him, and that our flesh profits nothing. He says the words that He speaks are spirit, and they are life, speaking of the truth. He confirms here the fact that man shall not live by bread alone, but by every word that proceed out of the mouth of God, which is the knowledge or truth of God's Word. We must be fed the Word of God in order to grow. It is our spiritual food.

The Apostle Peter, whom Jesus called to the Pastoral Ministry, was told by Jesus to feed His sheep in John 21:13-17, which says:

"Jesus then cometh, and taketh bread, and giveth them, and fish likewise. This is now the third time that Jesus showed himself to his disciples, after that he was risen from the dead. So when they had dined, Jesus saith to Simon Peter, Simon, son of Jonas, lovest thou me more than these? He saith unto him, Yea, Lord; thou knowest that I love thee. He saith unto him. Feed my lambs. He saith to him again the second time. Simon, son of Jonas, lovest thou me? He saith unto him, Yea, Lord; thou knowest that I love thee. He saith unto him, feed my sheep. He saith unto him the third time, Lovest thou me? And he (Peter) *said unto him, Lord, thou knowest all things; thou knowest that I love thee. Jesus saith unto him, Feed my sheep."* Jesus reveals to Peter at this time and to us all that the factor to obedience is love. If we truly loved Jesus, we would obey Him!

The Apostle Paul continues to specify what all we need to do to put off the old man which is corrupt according to the deceitful lusts.

He says:

*Wherefore **putting away lying**, speak every man truth with his neighbor: for we are members one of another. **Be ye angry, and sin not**; let not the sun go down upon your wrath: neither give place to the devil. Let him that stole*

The Cycle of Sin

steal no more: but rather let him labour, working with his hands the thing which is good, that he may have to give to him that needeth. **Let no corrupt communication proceed out of your mouth,** *but that which is good to the use of edifying, that it may minister grace unto the hearers, and grieve not the Holy Spirit of God, whereby ye are sealed unto the day of redemption.* **Let all bitterness,** *and* **wrath,** *and* **anger,** *and* **clamour,** *and* **evil speaking be put away** *from you, with* **all malice.** *And be ye kind one to another, tenderhearted,* **forgiving one another** *even as God for Christ's sake hath forgiven you. Be ye therefore followers of God, as dear children; and* **walk in love,** *as Christ also hath loved us, and hath given himself for us an offering and a sacrifice to God for a sweetsmelling savour. But* **fornication,** *and all* **uncleanness,** *or* **covetousness,** *let it not be once named among you, as becometh saints: Neither* **filthiness,** *nor* **foolish talking,** *nor* **jesting,** *which is not convenient: but rather give thanks. For this ye know, that no whoremonger, nor unclean person, nor covetous man, who is an idolater, hath any inheritance in the kingdom of Christ and of God* (Ephesians 4:25-32; 5:1-5)."

The devil's intent or aim is to keep us in darkness, or sin. If he can distract you and take your attention away from God, he has accomplished his objective. The devil will do everything to keep your attention away from God, away from the knowledge of the truth. Keep in mind, truth is the light of men (John 1:1-4; 14:6). Truth is what causes us to see. Jesus told the disciples concerning the religious leaders of His time, in John 15:22:

"If I had not come and spoken unto them, they had not had sin: but now they have no cloak for their sin."

Cloak, denotes covering, hidden from sight. Jesus exposed their sin of self-righteousness. Jesus is the light that came into a dark and wicked world. We are now the light of the world, those of us who have been born of the Spirit of God. Jesus tells us to let our light so shine. He says in Matthew 5:16:

"Let your light so shine before men, that they may see your good works, and glorify your Father which is in heaven."

Sin does not glorify God, obedience does. We are called to reflect Jesus Christ, to walk as Jesus did in love, humility, and in obedience to God. We can know we are walking in Victory because the truth exposes darkness (ignorance), and sin. In Galatians 5:19-21, sin is exposed, and says:

"Now the works of the flesh are manifest, which are these, Adultery, fornication, uncleanness, lasciviousness, Idolatry, witchcraft, hatred, variance, emulations, wrath, strife, seditions, heresies, Envyings, murders, drunkenness, revellings, and such like: of the which I tell you before, as I have told you in time past, that they which do such things shall not inherit the kingdom of God (Revelation 21:1-8)."

When we are walking in obedience or in Victory, we will bear fruit. Jesus said in John 15:3-12:

"Now ye are clean through the word which I have spoken unto you. Abide in me, and I in you. As the branch cannot bear fruit of itself, except it abide in the vine; no more can ye, except ye abide (continue) in me. I am the vine, ye are the branches: He that abideth in me, and I in him, the same bringeth forth much fruit: for without me ye can do nothing. If a man abide not in me, he is cast forth as a branch, and is withered; and men gather them, and cast them into the fire, and they are burned. If ye abide in me, and my words abide in you, ye shall ask (pray) what ye will, and it shall be done unto you. Herein is my Father glorified, that ye bear much fruit; so shall ye be my disciples. As the Father hath loved me, so have I loved you: continue ye in my love. If ye keep my commandments, ye shall abide in my love; even as I have kept my Father's commandments, and abide in his love. These things have I spoken unto you, that my joy might

remain in you, and that your joy might be full. This is my commandment, That ye love one another, as I have loved you (Love is the royal law and one of the laws of the kingdom of God)." Also, joy is the by-product of love. We can identify whether we are walking in the flesh, by the works of the flesh, or whether we are walking in the spirit, or being led by the Spirit of God by identifying the fruit of the Spirit in our lives. The Apostle Paul goes on in Galatians 5:22-25, and says:

"But the fruit of the Spirit is love, joy, peace, longsuffering, gentleness, goodness, faith, Meekness, temperance: against such there is no law (of sin and death). **And they that are Christ's have crucified the flesh with the affections and lusts**. If we live in the Spirit, let us also walk in the Spirit (of life in Christ Jesus)."

Why? "For ye were (once) sometime darkness, but now are ye light in the Lord: walk as children of light: (For the fruit of the Spirit is in all goodness and righteousness and truth☺ Proving what is acceptable unto the Lord. And have no fellowship with the unfruitful works of darkness, but rather reprove (expose) them. (Ephesians 5:8-11)." We are now children of light.

In 1 Peter 2: 9, it says: "But ye are a chosen generation, a royal priesthood, an holy nation, a peculiar people; that we should shew forth the praises of him (God) who hath called you out of darkness, into his marvellous light." We are called to walk no longer in darkness or sin, but in the light, or truth of God's Word.

David says in Psalm 119:105:

Thy word is a lamp unto my feet, and a light unto my path."

John also makes known that God is light, and says:

-8- Victory over Sin

"*This then is the message which we have heard of him, and declare unto you, that God is light, and in him is no darkness at all. If we say that we have fellowship with him, and walk in darkness* (sin), *we lie, and do not the truth: But if we walk in the light, as he is in the light, we have fellowship one with another, and the blood of Jesus Christ his Son cleanseth us from all sin* (1 John 1:5-7)." Sin has no power over those who are walking according to the Word of God. When you are walking in obedience, you are walking in Victory! When sin is controlling your life, you are living a defeated life. The Apostle John says in 1 John 2:3-6:

"*And hereby we do know that we know him, if we keep his commandments. He that saith, I know him, and keepeth not his commandments, is a liar, and the truth is not in him. But whoso keepeth his word, in him verily is the love of God perfected: hereby know we that we are in him. He that saith he abideth in him ought himself also so to walk, even as he walked.*"

Then, John the Apostle goes on also to say:

"*Beloved, let us love one another: for love is of God; and every one that loveth is born of God, and knoweth God. He that loveth not knoweth not God; for God is love. In this was manifested the love of God toward us, because that God sent his only begotten Son into the world, that we might live through him. Herein is love, not that we loved God, but that he loved us, and sent his son to be the propitiation for our sins. Beloved, if God so loved us, we ought also to love one another. No man hath seen God at any time. If we love one another, God dwelleth in us, and his love is perfected in us. Hereby know we that we dwell in him, and he in us, because he hath given us of his Spirit* (1 John 4:7-13.*"

I would like to leave you with one more passage of scripture. 1 John 5:1-5 says:

The Cycle of Sin

"WHOSOEVER BELIEVETH that Jesus is the Christ is born of God: and every one that loveth him that begat loveth him also that is begotten of him. By this we know we love the children of God, when we keep his commandments: For this is the love of God, that we keep his commandments: and his commandments are not grievous (burdensome). *For whatsoever is born of God overcometh the world: and this is the victory that overcometh the world, even our faith. Who is he that overcometh the world, but he that believeth that Jesus is the Son of God?*

Those who have truly come to know and love Jesus are obedient to God's Word. They through diligent prayer, fasting, giving, and studying have grown spiritually mature and are showing forth the reflection of who Jesus truly is.

The key to walking in Victory is to walk in obedience and love. Love is the factor to obeying God, intentional obedience. God has called us to love Him, one another, and even our enemies (Matthew 5:44). When you truly learn to love, and strive to become obedient to God and the command to love. You will have Victory over sin!

"Love worketh no ill to his neighbor: therefore love is the fulfilling of the law (Romans 13:10)."

Epilogue

Bonus Prophetic Teaching
From the Author

Basic Training in Spiritual Warfare

The Cycle of Sin

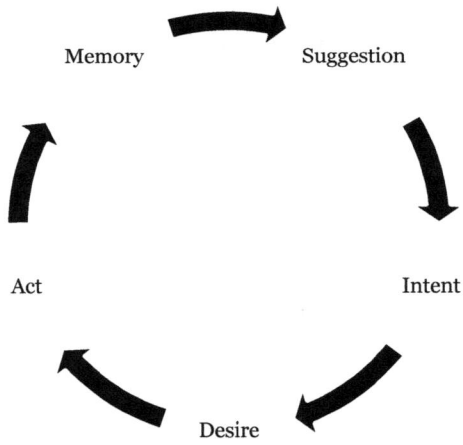

Memory → Suggestion

Act

Intent

Desire

-Epilogue-

Basic Training in Spiritual Warfare

*"Though we walk in the flesh, we do not war after the flesh:
(For the weapons of our warfare are not carnal, but mighty
through God to the pulling down of strongholds;)."*
2 Corinthians 10:3-4

<u>Our Enemies</u>

In Revelation 12:7-12, it lets us know in specific terms who our enemies are and says:

"And there was war in heaven: Michael and his angels fought against the dragon (satan*); and the dragon fought and his angels* (fallen*),   And prevailed not; neither was their place found any more in heaven* (the third). *And the great dragon was cast out, that old serpent, called the devil, and satan, which deceiveth the whole world: he was cast out into earth, and his angels were cast out with him."*

It goes on to say:

And I heard a loud voice saying in heaven, **Now is come salvation***, and strength,* **and the kingdom of our God***, and* **the power of his Christ***: for the accuser of our brethren is cast down, which accused them before our God day and night* (Zechariah 3:1; Job 1:6-12). *And they overcame him by the blood of the Lamb, and by the word of their testimony; and they loved not their lives unto death. Therefore rejoice, ye heavens, and ye that dwell in them* (the angels of God*). Woe to the inhabiters of the earth and sea! For the devil is come down unto you, having great wrath* (anger), *because he knoweth that he hath but a short time."*

Jesus confirms this account after having sent seventy of his disciples on a mission, and coming back from the mission scripture says:

"And then the seventy returned again with joy, saying, Lord, even the devils are subject unto us through thy name. And he (Jesus) said unto them, I beheld satan as lighting fall from heaven. Behold, I give you power to tread on serpents and scorpions and over all the power of the enemy; and nothing shall by any means hurt you. Notwithstanding in this rejoice not, that the spirits are subject unto you; but rather rejoice, because your names are written in heaven (Luke 10:17-20)."

These scriptures were given to show that the devil, and the fallen angels of the heavenlies, are now called unclean, wicked, foul, and evil spirits and now have access in the earth realm. The devil is angry because he knows that his time is short, and he is trying to take as many as he can to hell with him. When you see excessive anger in the heart of a person, it is what exposes the control of the devil in their life.

Ephesians 4:26 says:

"Be ye angry, and sin not: let not the sun go down upon your wrath: Neither give place to the devil."

We are not to allow anger to come into our hearts. The reason we are told this is because, anger in the heart gives place or opportunity to the devil, and it blinds us as with any other negative emotions that are not dealt with that lay dominant in our hearts, and when triggered will surface.

Proverbs 4:23 says:

"Keep (guard) *thy heart with all diligence; for out of it are the issues of life."*

Issues are subjects of concern, a source of conflict, misgiving, or emotional distress. Issues that are not dealt with or are unresolved will lay dominant in your heart, and when (tricked) or triggered will surface. It is called displaced emotions or aggression and over a period of time if accumulated will cause you to say or do something you otherwise would not have done. Aggression is the destruction that we see in the world today. I believe envy is the second wile of the devil (Proverb 14:30). The evil forces of satan will take hold of anger and ruin the very life of those who open that door to sin.

We must be aware that we are engaged in a spiritual war, and that our enemies are spiritual entities, which mean they are unseen. These unclean, wicked, foul, and evil spirits are everywhere. They are in our homes, in our workplaces, in our schools, and where ever people are you will find them. Unclean, wicked, foul and evil spirits inhabits whosoever they can. Whosoever opens themselves up to them they will inhabit. It is not hard to identify them, because they manifest their very nature.

The commander in chief of the power of darkness (the domain of the satan) is the devil and his unclean, wicked, foul, and evil spirits are his foot soldiers who are lesser in rank, than the principalities, powers, rulers of darkness and spiritual wickedness in high places. We are going to deals with the lesser entities, because they are the ones who we are confronted by in the earth realm, spiritual wickedness in high authority or places.

Spiritual warfare is implementing the Word of God in defeat of the enemy in our lives. When we obey the Word of God, we are walking in Victory! The Apostle Paul in these scriptures let us known that we are engaged in a spiritual war, he says that even though we walk in the flesh, or physical realm, we do not war after the flesh, for we have been given weapons that are not carnal or do not pertain to this world, but are mighty through God to the pulling down of strongholds.

-Basic Training in Spiritual Warfare-

If you are a Child of God, you are in the Army of the Lord, and Jesus Christ is your Commander in Chief! your identification is in Christ, who is the only begotten Son of God. But, we too are also sons and daughters of God through faith and as the Apostle Paul told Timothy to us also he says:

"No man (woman, boy or girl) warreth entangleth himself (herself) with the affairs of this life, that he (she) may please him who hath chosen him to be a soldier (2 Timothy 2:4)."

We are chosen of the Lord, and are told also not to entangle ourselves with the affairs of this life. What does it mean to be entangled with the affairs of this life? We entangle ourselves with the affairs of this life when we are depended on man, rather than God. The Apostle Paul also tells us like Timothy to endure hardship as a good soldier in the Lord. He says:

"THOU THEREFORE, my son (daughter), be strong in the grace that is in Christ Jesus. And the things that thou hast heard of me among many witnesses, the same commit thou to faithful men, who shall teach others also. Thou therefore endure hardness, as a good soldier of Jesus Christ."

The Battlefield

The battlefield is the mind. The war is waged in our minds through thoughts which are unseen, and spirit. We all know when we are being attack. But, only those who are able to detect or discern how the enemy specifically is coming against them are spiritually aware of the enemy's devices. 2 Corinthians 10:5, goes on to describe how the weapons of our warfare are able to pull down strongholds, by:

"Casting down imaginations, and every high thing that exalteth itself against the knowledge of God, and bringing into captivity every thought to the obedience of Christ;."

Strongholds are inroads of thoughts which have negatively

impacted the mind a person. An example: If you are continually being told you are ugly, you will believe you are ugly and likewise other words that attacks your mind or heart. Those thoughts that are spoken out of negativity are formed in the mind, and have become strongholds. The enemy targets our children, because they are too young to understand and are unaware of the spiritual attack on their minds. They see it as people being mean and evil. Spiritual warfare is a learned behavior which only the Holy Spirit can teach you to discern. We can make you aware of how the enemy is coming against you, and what he possibly is using to attack you. These strongholds were formed prior to your salvation in the Lord, Jesus Christ and as children because we were most vulnerable and unaware of spiritual things or the spiritual things of God. The enemy target children who are not properly loved, abused, and are mistreated by ungodly parents or people.

These unclean, wicked, foul, and evil spirits are of the main group. But, there are sub-grouping among them. I will use as an example the spirit of fear. The spirit of fear and other spirits enter in by way of the physical senses. The music industry is one way and the media is another way they use to enter through the ear and eye gates. The images of horror in movies impact the mind to where they instill fear within the individual. The spirit of fear builds a stronghold in the mind of its victim to bring fear against its victims which is subtle, and allows the spirit of fear to control the individual however it chooses. The spirit of fear causes the individuals to grow fond of watching such movies then torment them in subtle ways such as the displaying of the lack of confidence in oneself or having no motivation or initiative. Fear paralyzes its victim.

Now say, a stronghold of fear is within your mind. Rather than act in faith when you are face with diver situations or circumstances, you are fearful and allow fear to dominate your life. When circumstances deem the spirit of fear to manifest itself, it will through your thought process. You will begin to see, which is your imagination, what may appear to be an outcome of your situation or circumstance and it will cause you to become fearful. The spirit of fear and all other spirits attaches themselves to the individual's intellect and masquerades as part of their personality. Demon possession is different. They have control of your mind and the body.

Take an evil spirit for example, what is evil? Evil is a source of sorrow. An evil spirit causes sorrow. Evil spirits causes sorrow in the individual and towards others. Evil spirits injures people feelings, and causes them sorrow. Evil spirits also physically harm others. Among evil spirits are hatred, anger, malice, envy, jealousy, and covetousness. They are all spirits of deception. They all cause injury to the individual or others and are the wiles of the devil.

These unclean, wicked, foul, and evil spirits use people who have strongholds to attack other people. Who among the strongholds that is most harmful are the spirit of rejection, low self- esteem, inferior complex, and the more common ones are worry, anxiety, doubt, and unbelief. The stronghold of rejection is harmful in that it hinders the individual of receiving love, because he or she are guarding their hearts against being hurt or rejected. Along with the stronghold of rejection, you will find the spirit of anger. In self deliverance, the spirit of anger must be released by not giving in to it, and by submitting your will to God through your worship and praise!

When you know and understand the Word of God, it will help you to overcome the stronghold of rejection. Romans 5:8-9 says:

"But God commendeth his love toward us, in that while we were yet sinners, Christ died for us. Much more then, being now justified by his blood, we shall be saved from wrath through him. For if, when we were enemies, we were reconciled to God by the death of his Son, much more being reconciled, we shall be saved by his life (John 3:16)." We have

been accepted in the beloved (Ephesians 1:5-7). Jesus also teaches in Luke 21:16-19, that we would be rejected because of our faith in Him. He says: *"Settle it therefore in your hearts, not to meditate before what ye shall answer: For I will give you a mouth and wisdom, which all your adversaries shall not be able to gainsay nor resist. And ye shall be betrayed both by parents, and brethren, and kinfolks, and friends; and some of you shall they cause to be put to death. And ye shall be hated of all men for my name's sake. But there shall not an hair of your head perish. In your patience possess ye your souls."*   Jesus goes on to lets us know that He will never leave nor forsake us (Hebrews 13:5).

Our Weapons

The Apostle Paul tells us to put on the whole armour of God that we may be able to withstand in the evil day, or perilous times. Spiritual warfare is so extensive that before we can actually engage in spiritual warfare, we need to be trained to know and understand all of who we are. We need to know our true identity, that we are the Righteousness of God through faith in the Lord, Jesus Christ, and that we have been given weapons of our warfare, and these weapons given to us are spiritual weapons.

So the Apostle Paul says:

"Finally, my brethren, be strong in the Lord, and in the power of his might. Put on the whole armour of God that ye may be able to stand against the wiles of the devil. For we wrestle not against flesh and blood, but against principalities, against powers, against the rulers of the darkness of this world, against spiritual wickedness in high places (Ephesians 6:10-12)."

In the use of these weapons that are founded in Ephesians 6:13-18, it says:

-Basic Training in Spiritual Warfare-

"Wherefore take unto you the whole armour of God, that ye may be able to withstand in the evil day, and having done all, to stand. Stand therefore, having your loins girt about with truth, and having on the breastplate of righteousness; And your feet shod with the preparation of the gospel of peace; Above all, taking the shield of faith, wherewith ye are able to quench all the fiery darts of the wicked. And take the helmet of salvation, and the sword of the Spirit, which is the word of God: Praying always with all prayer and supplication in the Spirit, and watching thereunto with all perseverance and supplication for all saints."

Discernment is a gift given to the believer, we use to discern the attacks of the enemy. Discernment allows us as children of God to see, perceive and or understand spiritual things or the spiritual things of God.

What signals an attack? You learn to recognize an attack by three things. If someone liberally has taken something from you, if you are liberally being deprived of something that is rightly yours, and if something is trying to cause you spiritual or physical harm whether it be your person or property.

Jesus says in John 10:10:

"The thief cometh not, but for to steal, and to kill, and to destroy: I am come that they might have life, and that they might have it more abundantly."

Spiritual warfare is an attacks against our emotions, and one of the worst attack we are presently experiencing is the attack on our finances which causes the spirit of fear, worry, and anxiety to dominate the lives of those who are in the world, and God's people who are not trusting and depending on the Lord, Jesus Christ (Proverbs 3:5-6).

Again, spiritual warfare is much more extensive. We know that there are many books out on this subject, and their

-Epilogue-

teaching varies. So if you are interested in learning more, get familiar with what is being said, and then allow the Holy Spirit to give you discernment in this area. Just like salvation, which is personal. Spiritual warfare is personal, and is the work of the Holy Spirit to bring you awareness, and discernment. I wanted to just touch briefly on a few things. In due time, the Lord will allow me to complete a more extensive study on Spiritual Warfare. Remember, we are not fighting against one another, or flesh and blood. We are wrestling against unclean, wicked, foul, and evil spirit beings! We defeat the enemy by walking in the truth of God Word!

Warfare Prayers

#1

Heavenly Father,

Thank you for your Power and Strength. I am so thankful for the Armour you have provided me. I put on the Girdle of Truth, the Breastplate of Righteousness, the Sandals of Peace and the Helmet of Salvation. I lift up the Shield of Faith against all the fiery darts of the enemy; and I take in my hand the Sword of the Spirit, which is the Word of God against all the forces of evil in my life. I put on this Armour and live and pray in complete dependence upon you, Blessed Holy Spirit. I cover myself with the Blood of the Lord Jesus Christ as my Protection. I claim Victory, through my Lord and Savior, Jesus Christ. No Weapon that is form against me shall prosper. I bind every unclean, wicked, foul, and evil spirit hindering my walk with God, in the Name of Jesus. I plea the Blood of Jesus Christ against you satan, from the top of my head to the sole of my feet. To your Glory Father, in the Name of Jesus, Amen!

#2

Heavenly Father,

I Worship you and give you Praise. I recognize that you are worthy to receive all Glory and Honor and Praise. I renew my allegiance to you and pray that the Blessed Holy Spirit would enable me in this time of prayer. I am thankful, Heavenly Father that you sent the Lord Jesus Christ into the world to die as my substitute. I am thankful that the Lord Jesus Christ came as my representative and that through Him you have completely forgiven me; you have birth me into your family; you have assumed all responsibility for me; you have given me Eternal Life; you have given me the Perfect Righteousness of the Lord Jesus Christ so I am now Justified. I am thankful that in Him you have made me complete. In the Name of Jesus, Amen!

Warfare Prayers

#3

Heavenly Father,

Open my eyes that I might see how Great you are and how complete your provision is for this day. I am thankful that the Victory the Lord Jesus Christ won for me on the cross and in His resurrection has been given to me and that I am seated with the Lord Jesus Christ in the heavenlies and recognize by faith that all unclean, wicked, foul, and evil spirits and satan himself are under my feet. I declare, therefore, that satan and his unclean, wicked, foul, and evil spirits are subject to me in the Name of the Lord Jesus Christ. I renounce you satan, and command that you leave my presence with all of your demons. I take authority over my life, and rebuke any evil influence you may have against my life. I give myself to you Lord, completely. Give me Power to overcome satan in my life. Thank you Lord. In the Name of Jesus, Amen!

#4

Heavenly Father,

I bow in Worship and Praise before you. I cover myself with the Blood of the Lord Jesus Christ, as my Protection. I surrender my will completely and unreservedly in every area of my life to you. I take a stand against all the working of satan that would hinder me in my prayer life. I address myself only to you the True and Living God and refuse any involvement of satan in my prayer life. satan, I command you in the Name of the Lord Jesus to leave my presence with all your demons. I bring and plea the Blood of Jesus against and between us. Help me heavenly Father, to live my life pleasing to you. Give me the courage to say no to all that is not pleasing to you. Give me more compassion. Thank you heavenly Father, In the Name of Jesus, Amen!

Prayer Request Form

"Again I say unto you, That if two of you shall agree on earth as touching any thing that they shall ask, it shall be done for them of my Father with is in heaven."
Matthew 18:19

"And this is the confidence that we have in him, that, if we ask any thing according to his will, he heareth us; And if we know that he hear us, whatsoever we ask, we know that we have the petitions that we desired of him."
1 John 5:14-15

Let's stand on the promises of God!

Prayer Request:

_____

_____

_____

_____

_____

_____

Name_____
　　　　　　First　　　　　　　　　　Last

Address _____
　　　　　　　　　　　　City　　　　State　　Zip code

Copy and send to:

Minister Francine E. Shaw
P. O. Box 03600,
Highland Park, MI 48203

84

The Cycle of Sin

Contact:

You may call (313) 231-6836 or send your prayer request

to:

C/O Minister Francine E. Shaw
P.O. Box 03600
Highland Park, Michigan 48203

Or

E-mail to:

francineshawministries@yahoo.com

Please include contact information

Thank you!

About the Author

Francine Shaw is an Intercessor, Teacher, and an Evangelist of the New World Community Church, Detroit, Michigan. She is a certified member of International Chaplaincy Training Inc., where she serves as an Ordained Community Chaplain. She has been in ministry for 37 years, of which 10 years were in recovery, deliverance, and spiritual growth, and 27 years in training.

Her biblical perspective comes from her knowledge of God, and her actual experience of trusting and walking in the truth of God's Word. She is a Gulf War Veteran, and served in the Army National Guard for 11 years. God used her military training to teach her spiritual warfare, which enabled her to overcoming self, the practice of sin, and the strategies of the devil. Her God given vision is to establish an educational facility for the people of God for the sole purpose of spiritual growth and leadership development.

Francine Shaw contributes her leadership development to the late J. C. Powell, Founder of New World Community Church. The late Bishop Williams Hamilton France Sr., who ordained and trained her in the preaching of the Gospel of Jesus Christ, and Pastor Nathaniel Cotton Sr., who trained her in the Pastoral Ministries. All are great men of God.

To order additional copies of *The Cycle of Sin* or to find more life changing books by *ACTS PUBLISHING*, please contact.

Outreach at *Francine Shaw Ministeries*
P. O. Box 03600
Highland Park, MI 48203
actspublishing@yahoo.com

Or call
(313) 231-6836

Special discounts are available for ministry, academic, retail or fund-raising purposes.

www.ingramcontent.com/pod-product-compliance
Lightning Source LLC
LaVergne TN
LVHW021539080426
835509LV00019B/2731